Reviews of
Invite Joy Into Your Life

"Mary has created a treasure—a string of pearls, gathering one pearl at a time. Choose any one of the pearls—hold it, reflect with it, journal about it, live it, and be aware of the ripple effect in all of your being. Mary's words will be as a midwife for the birthing of joy in your living."

JEAN UMLOR, RSM, RN

"We are created for Joy! Mary Seger gives complete, practical, helpful ways to be joyful.

A treasure chest for joy. Choose a chapter—all are helpful for your well-being as a woman.

Accept the invitation to experience Joy! Mary Seger gives an affirming way to live Joy.

I found many helpful ways to keep joy in my daily life."

JOANN M. FURY, Spiritual Director

"Joy is about the choices we make and the wisdom and courage to make them. Mary Seger leads the reader through many positive avenues which can enhance Life with Joy."

SHEILA QUINN SIMPSON, author of
Apology: The Importance and Power of Saying "I'm Sorry"

Invite
Joy Into
Your Life

Steps for Women Who Want to
Rediscover the Simple Pleasures of Living

Mary B. Seger, NP, PhD

Sophia Rose
Press

Published by Sophia Rose Press
P. O. Box 1924
Gaylord, MI 49734
www.maryseger.com

PUBLISHER'S CATALOGING-IN-PUBLICATION DATA
Seger, Mary B.
    Invite joy into your life: steps for women who want to rediscover the simple pleasures of living / Mary B. Seger — Gaylord, Mich. : Sophia Rose Press, 2007.

    p. ; cm.
    ISBN-13: 978-0-9790461-0-0
    Includes bibliographical references and index.

    1. Joy. 2. Happiness. 3. Women—Mental health. 4. Women—Conduct of life. I. Title.

BF575.H27 S44 2007   2007920051
152.4/2—dc22   200701

Printed in the United States of America
10 9 8 7 6 5 4 3 2

Poetry on pages 16, 118, and 237 by Sandra Hines

Watercolor artwork on cover by Alma Harrison

Interior and cover design by To The Point Solutions
www.tothepointsolutions.com

To my daughter,
Stephanie Rose Noss.
You are my greatest joy!

Contents

Contents

Preface

♡

Are there days when you don't want to get out of bed, it seems as though life has lost its luster and you wonder what is the point? Do you not feel quite right—but you can't figure out what's wrong?

I am a nurse practitioner with a PhD in natural health. In my integrative medicine practice I treat women with a variety of illnesses and ailments, although lately it seems that a large part of my time is spent counseling patients on how to reduce stress and invite joy into their lives.

I strongly believe that eating well and getting regular exercise is imperative to good health and a positive attitude. And for some individuals, traditional medicine is required as they begin to make healthy changes in their lives.

What I have also discovered, however, is no matter how well you eat; how much you exercise; how many herbs and supplements you take; or how many alternative practitioners you see for healing, if you don't have joy in your life you will still feel like something is amiss. You will have mornings when you'd rather stay in bed than start your day.

Health is as much an "inside" job as it is a physical one. When women take responsibility for their health and make changes in their lives, magic occurs. I have seen this in my practice, and it is such a blessing to witness the awesome transformation of someone who has made changes and returned joy to her life. She comes alive—as a woman, a mother, a daughter, a wife!

Although I have encouraged women to invite joy into their lives for many years, it took a chance opportunity for me to embrace the necessity of having joy in one's life. A friend of mine was asked to give a speech on joy, but had a schedule conflict. Since I had spoken on a variety of health issues for the last ten years, she asked if I would take her place. It sounded interesting, so I agreed.

As I researched the subject of joy, I found little information. So, I looked more closely at my life and the lives of my patients. What I found was a preponderance of joylessness. This made me sad—until I realized that I could teach women how to get joy, pleasure, and passion in their lives.

I gave the speech and the feedback was encouraging— women soaked up the information on how to incorporate positive changes into their daily lives and thereby feed their bodies, minds, and souls.

This book contains the information I presented at that speech and others that followed.

Acknowledgments

This book would not have been written except for the many special people who help me live my life in joy.

Thank you to my daughter, Stephanie Rose Noss, my greatest joy. I am blessed to have you in my life.

Thank you to my brothers, Brad, Craig, Clark, and Wayne, for the fun, laughter, and advice we have shared over the years. I am also grateful for your wives, my sisters-in-law, Vikki, Karri, and Danielle. I thank you for the love, support, and joy you have given me.

Thank you to my nieces and nephews, for bringing light and joy into my life: Shanna, Stephen, Sarah, Sarina, Sharissa, Zachery, Bradley, Josie, Jake, Elyssa, Catherine, Gwendolyn, Zoltan, and Craig.

Terry, thank you. I couldn't get through life without you. Your wisdom has led me back to my joy and made me laugh out loud too many times to count.

Acknowledgments

Thank you Sandra and Wendy, for staying with me through the ups and downs of life. Your compassion and wisdom have helped return me to my path of joy.

Thank you Debbie, for asking me to fill in for your speaking engagement and thereby sparking my interest in joy.

Thank you to Jan and Christopher, who have held me accountable in pursuing my dreams and making them a reality. Also, thank you for reminding me to laugh and count my blessings.

Thank you to Sandy, Meri Jo, and Marcia, for your support and for cheering me on in my work and personal lives.

Thank you to Lydia, Deb, and Vikki, for always reminding me to make those intentions and to believe.

Thank you to Cheryl, for the support, wisdom, and practical advice you have shared with me over the years.

Thank you Monika, for all the healing energy you have provided over the years, and the pointed reminders to let my light shine. You are a blessing!

Thank you to my patients, for sharing your joys and sorrows with me. It has been a great honor to bear witness to your lives.

Thank you to Grandma Rose, Sister Jean, and the many wise women who guided me to invite joy into my life in such loving and compassionate ways.

Thank you to Mary Jo Zazueta, for taking my words and making them into this book. What an incredible process it has been.

Thank you to Jean Parker, for taking the ideas in my head and my scribbles and making them into such incredible works on paper. You make it so much fun!

Last but not least, thank you to my dog, Keisha, for being a bundle of joy and for your unconditional love.

Introduction

♡

The *American Heritage Dictionary* defines joy as "a condition or feeling of high pleasure or delight." I define joy as the warm feeling that starts in the center of your chest and gradually spreads down to your toes and up to the top of your head. It is the warm feeling you get when you hold a puppy, a kitten, or an infant. It is a tremendous feeling—and its absence makes for a dire life.

Wishing or wanting improvement or change in your life is not enough. You will have to do something to get results. It takes action to bring joy into your life.

In the following chapters, you will find a number of steps you can take to bring joy into your life. Find one that resonates with you and work on it for a week or two. Place Post-it notes throughout your home and office to remind you of what you're working on. Focus on one activity at a time and then move onto the others as your mood and life dictate.

Everyone is different—work on what *your* body, mind, and spirit need. Continue working your way through these exercises until joy and passion are a part of your daily life. It won't happen overnight and there may be days when you feel little or no joy, but there will be times when you dance through the day. Keep on doing the activities and know that the more you practice the better you will feel.

Many times when women begin to do what is important to them they encounter an incredible number of obstacles. Their belief is that because of all the obstacles, they are not meant to do what is important to them, so they go back to serving others. Wrong!! This is a test; it is only a test. You are meant to invite joy into your life and find the simple pleasures of life.

Imagine this: you are at the bottom of a hill. At the top of this hill you know there is a spectacular view and you are excited about seeing this view. You know it will bring you great joy and pleasure. You begin climbing the hill. After you are about halfway up the hill you realize it takes much time and effort to reach the summit. Do you say to yourself: "This is hard work. I am not worth it. I do not deserve to see the spectacular view and bring joy and pleasure into my life"? Do you then turn around and retreat down the hill and return to serving others? Or do you say: "This is hard work but I am worth it. I can do this. I will sit here and rest for a while, gather my strength, and then forge on. I will see this spectacular view. I will invite joy into my life and enjoy the simple pleasures of living"? This book will help you choose the second scenario.

Before you begin reading, define what joy *feels* like to you. Is it warmth in your heart or is it smiling uncontrollably? However you feel joy, write it down.

What gives you joy? Is it being with people, taking a walk, or doing a favorite activity? The exercises in this book will help you define what brings you joy and how to get it back in your life. In contrast, this book also helps you identify the "joy snatchers" in your life and gives you ideas on how to eradicate them. No matter how much joy you are able to bring into your life, if you don't work on removing the joy snatchers, your work will be for naught.

As you work through the steps and rediscover joy, you may want to revisit some of the chapters. Maintaining joy in your life is a continuous process. As you learn more about yourself, what snatches your joy, and how to invite joy into your life, you will open yourself up to a whole new world of simple pleasures.

Commit to yourself that you will make time each day to work through these chapters. Until you are whole in body, mind, and spirit you will suffer—and so will those around you.

Invite Joy Into Your Life is about moving forward—about taking steps. It is not about looking back and beating yourself up for what you have done or have failed to do. You cannot change the past, you can only do work in the present, which can then change your future. So, throw away the big stick, grab a journal and a pretty pen, and let's get started.

THE CALL OF JOY

As joy came
Tripping by one day,
She smiled and called,
"Come on let's play."

I shook my head
And said "Oh no,
I have to work,
So go away."

She grinned and chuckled
And hung around.
No gloomy Gus
Could get her down.

She showed her self
In many ways
In velvet kisses
From sun's warm rays

In tickled cheeks
From tender breezes,
In bright blue skies
And sudden sneezes.

So many ways she
Called my name,
I finally grinned
And turned her way.

So now we laugh
And whisper too,
She calls to all,
She calls to you.

~ SANDRA HINES

ONE

This Little Light of Mine

♡

This little light of mine, I'm going to let it shine . . ." Do you remember this song from your childhood? When was the last time you let your light shine?

My assistant makes incredible glass beads that she strings together into beautiful bracelets. The jewelry she creates is awesome and you can tell this is work she was meant to do. The other day she came into the office and showed me a letter of acceptance into a juried art show. She was aglow all day.

Yesterday a patient said to me, "I love your bracelet . . . a friend of mine gave me some beads that look like those." My assistant found out that her friend had purchased the beads from her and given them to the patient. Of course, the patient raved about how much she loved the beads. My assistant was dumbfounded, "She really likes my beads!"

With easy reassurance, I commented on the beautiful art she creates. She responded with, "I forget that sometimes," and then her light came on. I love when that happens.

Your light is your joy. It's the warmth that fills you up when you feel great, content, happy. When your light is on, it casts a glow on everyone around you. That one little light heals you and others who feel the warmth. When you let your light shine, you impact the people near you, which then impacts even more people. This is how we begin to change the world; not by changing others, but by finding our lights and letting them shine.

Was your light allowed to shine when you were a child? Can you see lights in the children around you, or have they been stamped out?

I will never forget my daughter's kindergarten teacher. She had the most incredible light. I watched as the children went up to the front of the classroom to tell her something. She would kneel down to their level and focus on that child. Their lights glowed and the looks of love that they gave to their teacher were an inspiration to see. What an incredible way to begin one's school years.

Do you allow children to let their lights shine? I think society stamps out the light in children around age eleven or twelve. Is it hormonal? I don't think so. I think it is society's way of saying you must be serious, you must be responsible, and you must work. No time for that light-shining business. And so, the light goes out until you realize that something is very wrong with your life.

I also believe that life's hard knocks can build up brick walls around your heart and then you stop allowing your light to shine out of fear. Those brick walls can lead to a lot of heart, breast, and lung problems.

When you don't allow your light to shine, you shut down the heart's emotional center or heart *chakra*. This is where you feel joy; this is where you feel love. When you feel joy and love your light is on. When you don't, your light is snuffed out. You build up emotional walls that you believe will protect you from further pain, yet all they do is shut out your light.

Another way to slowly dim your light is to give love while not accepting love in return. I see this with women all the time. A phenomenon I have noticed lately is normal systolic blood pressure (the top number) with high diastolic blood pressure (the bottom number). The diastolic number is related to the circulation of the heart. It means there is more pressure in the heart instead of a free and easy flow of blood. I have started talking to my patients about this.

I saw a massage therapist the other day who had a normal systolic blood pressure and a high diastolic blood pressure. I asked, "When someone says thank you for their massage, do you feel the thank you or do you just brush it off?" From the look on her face I knew she just brushed it off. I asked her to practice letting the thank-yous and gifts of love in, and then monitor what happened to her blood pressure. I also said, "You do give an awesome massage and it is time to accept that into your heart." Boy, did her light come on. We'll see what happens with her blood pressure as she begins to accept the gifts of love.

Do you accept love into your heart? Take a moment to think about the last time someone said thank you or I love you to you. Take a deep breath in and out. Take another deep breath in, and as you inhale let that love come into your heart. Feels pretty good, doesn't it? It may even bring a tear to your eye. It may bring a lot of tears, as your heart fills with the love and light it was meant to feel.

19

Unfortunately, some people are threatened by your light and strive to put it out. A patient in her sixties was talking about her mother who was in her eighties. Her mother was not doing well and this woman needed to figure out how she could get some help for her mother. Her sister lived near their mother, but could not help. I asked why not. My patient explained that her mother could put her sister in a fetal position in a short amount of time.

What a powerful statement about the effect others, especially those closest to you, can have. Has this happened to you? You are dancing through your day, when all of a sudden an attack comes out of nowhere and your light goes out. Or worse, how about those days when you come home and yell at the kids, scream at the dog, and feel just miserable? Yuck! When your light is out you have the ability to put other people's lights out too.

This is just as powerful as your ability to warm people when your light is on. You have a choice, to keep your light on or allow it to be turned off and stay off. You can say: "I will let my light shine and not allow anyone to put it out."

Where is that little light inside of you? Is it buried deep within your heart? Is it ready to come out and shine? It is time. It is time to find your light and let it shine, no matter what. It is time to feel joy and let the light shine through when you are doing something you love. It is time to feel childlike wonderment for this world and let your light shine. It is time to look at others with your light on and let them feel the light of your love.

It is especially time for you to let love from others into your heart, so you can shine brighter. It is time for you to look at your relationships and question them.

Do the relationships in your life turn out your light or allow you to shine? It is time to stop letting people put out your light.

How do you do this? You focus on the relationships and people that let you shine. Those that try to put out your light are simply tests, lessons, or experiences that ask you to honor yourself. It is easy to fall into a trap and believe that if someone says you are worthless you must be; if they don't love you, you must be unlovable. Not true. It is time you believe you are a worthwhile, incredibly awesome, loveable human being— and let your light shine.

Neale Donald Walsch wrote a children's book entitled *The Little Soul and the Sun*. (He also wrote the *Conversations with God* series.) It is a story about angels and The Little Soul that wants to feel what it is like to be the Light. Sometimes the only way you can find your light is when you are in darkness and realize you are the light and you deserve to let your light shine. "Rather be a Light unto the darkness. Then you will know Who You Really Are, and all others will know, too. Let your Light so shine that everyone will know how special you are!" It is a wonderful book to read to yourself and your children.

"This little light of mine, I'm going to let it shine . . ."

How are you going to let your light shine from this day forward?

EXERCISES

Before the week is out, you must do something that brings you joy, so you can feel the light shining within you. Write about how it feels to experience joy. If you can, awaken the feeling inside of you, let your light shine, and then look in a mirror. You will be truly glorious to behold. Write about how it feels to see yourself with your light on.

For one week find seven different people to shine your light on. Let your light shine through your eyes, feel it in your heart, and direct it towards them. It can be done with a smile, a thank you, or by saying I love you. Each day, write down whom you shined your light on, how you felt, and if you saw a difference in that person.

Accept a thank you and/or love that is directed to you from someone else. It doesn't matter whom you choose to experience this with, but you must do it fully and completely. You may use a memory to do this, however the exercise will have greater impact if you use a new experience. Let the feelings of love and appreciation flow into your heart. Tears may come, but do not stop the experience. Let the love stay in your heart. Write about how this feels.

Write about how you felt when you were with a person or group that encouraged your light to shine. How can you get together with this person or people more often?

Write about the people who put you in a fetal position. Write about how you will say: "No more! I will move away from you and let my light shine." Then, do it.

And as we let our own light shine,
we unconsciously give other people
permission to do the same.

Marianne Williamson

TWO

Solitude

Many people do not like the idea of solitude. They equate solitude with being alone, which can lead to loneliness and thoughts like "nobody likes me." Everyone wants to be loved and needed; however, we often think that being loved and needed must come from outside of ourselves—from someone else. But that is not the case. These feelings *must* come from inside you, and the way to find this love, this person inside of you, is to find solitude.

Solitude brings you face to face with yourself, which can be unsettling as you gain insight into your life. It is sometimes easier to continue running away from yourself by helping others, or whatever you do to stay busy, rather than take the time for you.

When you finally stop and find solitude, listen. You might realize you haven't been taking very good care of yourself.

Women often find it difficult to take care of themselves. We put ourselves so low on our priority lists that we never get around to us. We then wonder why we are so unhappy and angry. Women often tell me: "My life is great. What is wrong with me?"

"Who are you? What do you want?" I ask. They usually do not know because they have never taken the time to ask the question, let alone listen for the answer.

In *Women Who Run With the Wolves*, Clarissa Pinkola Estés, PhD, defines solitude as "the cure for the frazzled state so common in modern women . . . a way of listening to the inner self to solicit advice and guidance otherwise impossible to hear in the din of daily life." We rarely take the time in solitude to listen for the answers to the questions we ask. It is time to make time.

Solitude is being "far from the madding crowd". It is a time to ask questions and listen for the answers. Sometimes the answers come slowly, as your self is not accustomed to being heard.

Answers can come as a quiet thought, a gut reaction, or a feeling of inspiration. Journaling your thoughts and questions can help you find the answers. As you write about how you feel, inspiration can occur. Another journaling technique that is successful is writing three pages every morning when you wake up. This technique is discussed in the books *The Artist's Way* and *Walking in this World*, both by Julia Cameron. (I highly recommend these books as tools to use to discover the inner you.)

One of my favorite ways to find answers is to go to a bookstore and browse. Eventually I pick up a book that looks interesting. I hold it between the palms of my hands, take a deep breath, and silently ask a question. I then open it up and read the passage. I am amazed at the answers I have received. I now have several books I found in this way.

A patient recently told me she was struggling with deciding whether to go back to work or stay home with her children. For inspiration, she opened her *Woman's Devotional Bible*. The lesson for the day was "Who Will Teach the Children," which was about a mother who had returned to her job. She was working so many hours her children began to suffer, so she ended up resigning. My patient received her answer.

Another fun way to get answers is by using oracle cards. These cards depict angels, animals, or fairies. My favorite deck is "Healing with the Angels" by Doreen Virtue, PhD. They contain beautiful images of angels and come with a booklet that explains the meaning of each card. I use these cards when I am feeling distressed or when I have a question. The process of using the cards not only gives me a message, but it is also calming.

I always sit in my comfortable chair and center myself by taking a few deep, relaxing breaths. As I shuffle the deck I focus on my question, which may even be a request for help. After I have shuffled for a while I set the cards down and cut the deck with my left hand, then turn over the card where I cut the deck. I look at the top card and see what feelings and thoughts come up. These are my gut feelings and the true answer to my question or concern. Looking up the card in the booklet can also bring more clarity. It seems the more I play with the cards, the clearer the answers are that I receive.

Reading, journaling, playing with oracle cards, and letting your mind roam are activities that can be done in solitude to help you find your true self. If you are searching, solitude is imperative to help you find the answers.

"I don't have time for myself," is a cry I hear many times

each day in my office. If you say this, the reality is you are not ready to make changes and/or your life is not yet bad enough to push you to make changes. The time will come, however, when you can no longer tolerate the emptiness that you feel—or you will get sick. Trust me, if you scheduled time in for yourself *before* that happens, it is so much easier.

Of course, many women wonder how they are supposed to find time for solitude. For most of us, it must be written into our schedules, in ink. Select a time of day that works best for you. Then schedule an hour of "me time." It will be pure bliss.

Solitude can be found in many places. I love to go to Lake Michigan and walk the beach and watch and listen to the water. I also enjoy the drive to the lake. I listen to music, inspirational tapes, or let my mind wander. I find solitude and peace as I drive down the highway, though not when there is a lot of traffic.

Going out of town alone is a wonderful way to find quiet time and get to know yourself. Traveling to conferences offers me this opportunity. Flying offers a significant amount of time to read a book or catch up on rest. When was the last time you ate in silence or had several evenings to yourself? It sounds scary, but as you get used to being with yourself, it can be enlightening.

If you are not used to being alone, how do you do it without freaking out? As the Nike commercial says: "Just do it!" But do it in baby steps. Try waking up fifteen minutes early and doing the techniques we've discussed. On some mornings you may want to journal and ask the question, "Where else can I find solitude?" As the ideas come, write them down; and then make the time for solitude outside your home each week.

Many people are unable to relax in their homes, let alone find solitude. There is always so much to do; there are too many diversions to relax. It is time you change this! When you take fifteen minutes of solitude, look around and appreciate the home you have. If you live in chaos, however, you may only be able to appreciate the roof over your head and the few moments of silence you have found. Appreciate what you can, and look for more things to appreciate.

Another way to relax in your home is to be in the present moment. "I am here right now, and I am not worried about the future or the past." Plant your feet on the ground, be in the present moment, and breathe.

EXERCISES

Explain what solitude means to you.

Gather the items you will use during your times of solitude and place them in a box that is easily accessible on a daily basis, i.e., your favorite CDs, a book, or angel cards. Write about what you gathered.

Spend fifteen minutes a day in solitude—either in silence or with music. How did it feel the first time? How did it feel the tenth time? Write about each experience.

Make a list of places outside of your home where you can find solitude. Visit one per week.

Dream about a place you can visit and stay overnight or for several days. Then plan how you can make this dream a reality. Write about this place.

As you get comfortable with being in solitude, practice letting your light shine. The next time you are in solitude, take a moment to think about something that brings you joy. As you do this, feel your light shining, feel the joy flowing through your body, and feel the healing power of letting your light shine. Write about how this feels.

♡

Solitude is a willful choice of being alone—a time of reflection and introspection. There is exhilaration of the spirit and ecstasy of the mind. It is good for the Soul.

Charlotte Bottoms

THREE

Find a Comfort Spot

A few years ago, I co-taught a class on *Soul Comfort*. One of the first assignments was for each woman to find her comfort spot, a place where she could go when she needed to find consolation. It was also where she was to do her work for the class: reading, journaling, and dreaming.

One divorced woman was thrilled to realize she had made her entire house a comfort spot. Her home was filled with the colors and items she loved. She was happy to realize how far she had come from the cold house she shared with her ex-husband to the warm, comfortable home in which she now lives.

If you already have a comfort spot, great. If not, take time to consider the possibilities. Maybe it's your bedroom or a spare room, where you can shut the door and have quiet time. Or it may be a soft chair in the living room. The main goal is that the spot you select feels comfortable to you—and is yours.

Sometimes it is fun to quickly whip something together; then it is done and you can use it. However, with this project, act slowly. Take time. You may find a color you like, but as you look further, you find one you love even more. Use your judgment and make this a special place.

Imagine how you want your comfort spot to look. What colors would you like around you? What type of chair or other furniture do you see? Do you want a whole room for your comfort spot—or just a special chair? What would you do to change the room to make it yours?

A soft chair and blanket are essential for any comfort spot. If you don't have a special chair, start dreaming about one. Save your change and dollar bills. Look in magazines and catalogues for that perfect chair. When you find it, cut it out, and focus on the fact that you will have the chair one day. (It is amazing how things happen once you believe they are possible.)

I was recently in a furniture shop when I spotted a chaise lounge. The colors in it would blend perfectly in my living room. My first thoughts were I didn't need any more furniture and I couldn't have a chaise lounge in the living room. Still, I decided to sit in it—and it was heavenly. It fit me perfectly for sitting, and was even better lying down for a nap. Did I buy it? Not yet.

But I did get the catalogue and cut out the picture and put it in my journal. I think about it occasionally and can see myself lounging on it. (And, my friends told me that if I wanted a chaise lounge in my living room, I could have a chaise lounge in my living room. I love my friends.)

For those of you who already have a comfort spot, good for you. Is there any way you would like to modify it to make it more comfortable? I already had my spot in the living room when I redecorated my home. However, this past year I moved the furniture around and now I look outside instead of at the wall. This has added a new dimension to my spot. (Cleaning the windows this spring is next on my list.)

If you don't have a spot, there is no hurry. Dream and look for what you really want. You can set up a temporary place until you are ready for a permanent one. Be patient and know that what you want will come to you. Enjoy the spot you have and let go of any frustration caused by not being settled.

We are always in such a hurry to complete something so we can move on to what's next. We forget to be grateful for what we have. Take time to enjoy your temporary spot and keep focusing on your permanent spot. It will come to you when the time is right.

Women need a comfort spot because it is part of their nesting instinct. And, this need for personal space appears to get stronger as women age. I believe women feel a strong desire to change their home to one that is comfortable for them. When women are younger, we provide a nest for our husbands and/or children and we are busy with our careers and don't have time for *our* home. As we get older, our femininity starts to come out and we change our environment to reflect it.

Have you found your tastes changing? Do you feel the need to alter your environment? Women need to be surrounded by things that are pleasing to the eye, that are comfortable, and that bring them pleasure. It fills us up and allows us to love those around us from a place of fullness.

Are you going to get any support for making changes to your home? Some women may, but many won't. Support can range from having your husband build you an art studio to "Well, honey, if that's what you want," to "You are *not* changing *anything* in this house, we can't afford it." Start small with your comfort spot. It is a sacred space that is meant just for you. You need to revert back to your two-year-old self and say "Mine!" and mean it. Whether it is a chair or a room, the people in your home need to know that this is *your* spot. They may only use it when you invite them, though I suggest not extending an invitation.

Why? Do you want other people's stuff crowding and eventually taking over your comfort spot? You know that will happen. You're just setting boundaries. Imagine this: it's been a long day. You are ready to go to your comfort spot and read for a while. You have been looking forward to it all day and you deserve it. You make yourself a cup of tea and can feel a sense of peace enveloping you. You round the corner into the room where your comfort chair is, but what do you see? Your daughter sitting in the chair, eating potato chips, reading, and jamming to music on her headphones. It is a jarring sight; the peaceful feeling quickly leaves you. Just as you are about to yell, your child looks up at you and says, "Hi, Mom!" with a big smile on her face. You ask her, in a calm voice, to please get out of your chair, and then you snuggle into your comfort spot. This is yours. This is your comfort spot.

Several women who have taken possession of a spare room for their comfort spot, ask me if they ever have to come out. I laugh and tell them if they find themselves shopping for a small refrigerator and a hotpot, there could be a problem. Then I assure them that as they take time for themselves, every day, in their comfort spot, they will be able to come out, and eventually will want to come out.

I also suggest time-outs. When you are having a bad day and all you seem to be doing is yelling at your children or anyone else who gets in your way, you can stop and announce, "I need a time-out" and go to your comfort spot. (As any good woman knows, time-out is a punishment, so you should not be skipping with joy as you head off for a short time-out.)

You may want to apply the rule I used with my daughter. She spent a minute in time-out for each year of her age, i.e., five minutes when she was five years old. You could be gone for a long time. Enjoy!

EXERCISES

Walk around your house and start looking for a comfort spot. Sit in some chairs, get comfy in your bed, and look around. How does it feel? Try another spot and see how that one is. Write down what feels right about a couple of different locations.

Does your comfort spot need anything? Paint? New curtains? Write down what you would like to add (or remove) to your comfort spot.

Are you considering taking over a room? Write about how you would like the room to look. Get paint chips, cut out pictures from magazines, etc. You can even make a collage of your dream room.

Browse through magazines and decorating brochures. What catches your eye? Watch TV programs on redecorating. Write down any interesting ideas.

Who will support you in making the necessary changes to acquire a comfort spot? Do you need physical help or just emotional? For some women, taking back a piece of their home is a big step in setting boundaries. Get all the help you can. Write down who will assist you and how.

You may want to cut out pictures of what you want and paste them in your journal.

Once your comfort spot is ready, take a photo of it and tape it in your journal—or better yet, have someone take a photo of you in your comfort spot. Congratulations! Enjoy!!

Now that you have a comfort spot, practice using it for solitude. If you have a comfort room, you can be in solitude anytime. Simply close the door and attach a Do Not Disturb sign to the doorknob. (You may need to explain to your family that knocking on the door is included under "do not disturb.") Now, take a moment, breathe, and feel the joy coursing through your body. Ahhhh!

There is nothing like staying at home for real comfort.

Jane Austen

FOUR

Breathing and Meditation

When was the last time you took a deep cleansing breath? Have you ever? Most people take shallow breaths or hold their breath when they are stressed. This is not good. When you don't take in enough air, your body can't function well. Your muscles get tense, which can cause pain in the neck, shoulders, and lower back.

Breathing deeply completely relaxes your muscles. Take a deep breath in through your nose, hold it, and then breathe out of your mouth. How did that feel? Now, close your eyes, put your hands on your lower belly, and take a deep breath in through your nose. Hold it and then breathe out through your mouth. Did you feel your belly rise as you took a breath in and fall as you let your breath out? You may not have, as most people don't breathe properly. They are so intent on holding their abdominal muscles in or just too tense, they never take full deep breaths.

Sometimes breathing deeply is easier when lying down, so try that. Lie on the floor or on your bed and bend your knees. Place a rolled up hand towel underneath your neck to straighten your spine. Take a few moments to let the muscles of your back and shoulders relax into the floor. Doesn't this feel great? This is a wonderful relaxing technique for lower-back, neck, and shoulder pain. Now, close your eyes and place your hands on your belly. Take a deep breath in through your nose, hold it for a moment, and release your breath through your mouth. Do you feel your belly rising when you breathe in and falling when you breathe out? Keep practicing until you do. (If you have pets or small children it is best to do this exercise behind closed doors.)

Once you are comfortable with the technique of breathing in and out and having your belly rise and fall while lying down, focus on the experience. In time, it will feel like bliss. As you take deep breaths you will feel your muscles relax and maybe even a tingle all the way down to your toes. Pure joy!

Once you have mastered the art of breathing, it is time to put it to practical use. Pay attention to the shallow breathing you do throughout the day and to the times when you are actually holding your breath. As you catch yourself doing this, take a deep breath or two and focus on how good this change feels.

When you are in a stressful situation, take a moment and breathe fully. In most stressful situations it may not be appropriate to lie on the floor and take deep breaths—but you *can* take a slow, quiet breath in through your nose and let it out through your nose, with your eyes open. You will want to do this softly so it doesn't disturb the people around you—which takes practice.

When you have ten things to do and only enough time for five, say to yourself: "I have all the time I need" and then take a deep breath. As soon as you do this, your inner critic will clearly state: "No, you do not have enough time to accomplish everything you want to; you only have time to do five things." This will immediately cause shallow breathing and your neck, shoulders, and back muscles to tense. You then repeat: "I have all the time I need" and take a deep breath. Keep doing this over and over.

After you have practiced this many times, your inner critic may start to think you know what you are talking about and leave you alone. Eventually you will be amazed at what you can accomplish in the amount of time you have. You will be relaxed and focused on what needs to get done instead of stressed out about what you can't do. You will have more energy and thus accomplish more. Tension takes a tremendous amount of energy. The next time you are stressed about all that you have to do, try this technique and see what happens.

Another opportunity to use this breathing technique is during meditation. To meditate you need to find a chair or spot on the floor, sit down, get comfortable, close your eyes, and focus on your breath. Sounds pretty simple, doesn't it? It is.

As you sit, concentrate on breathing in and out. Your mind will take off in a hundred different directions. Gently bring your thoughts back to your breathing, and breathe in and breathe out. It is important to realize that your brain does not want to focus on your breathing, so if you only get a few seconds of quiet at first, that is awesome. Just keep practicing. The goal is to clear your mind and relax—for as long as possible.

It is interesting to note how meditation affects your life, not just the minutes you are actually meditating. Even though you might not spend much time in meditation, the side effects will positively affect your whole day. When you meditate on a regular basis, it will affect your life. Things will not stress you out as often or as much as they used to.

Something I learned from studying with Deepak Chopra is that you can make a list of intentions or prayers to read before you meditate. Write your intentions in the "I am" format. For example: "I am eating well, exercising daily, enjoying life, and finding enlightenment" or "I am helping my daughter with her homework in a loving and gentle manner" or "I have found the perfect black dress."

The intentions or prayers must be about you. For example, intending your daughter to do her homework in a happy mood is not as effective as saying you will help her in a loving manner. You can't change someone else's behavior, only your perception of their behavior. The more frequently you ponder your intentions, you will see yourself moving towards manifesting what you want.

Write your intentions in a notebook and put the date by the intention when it manifests itself in reality. Rewrite them and add to them periodically, as needed. It is a simple process of believing that anything is possible, and letting your wishes and desires come true.

Guided meditations are helpful in controlling the mind when you first start to meditate. Andrew Weil has developed an informative and helpful CD called Breathing, The Master Key to Self-Healing. He talks about why breathing is important, then takes you through various breathing techniques. Susie Levan's Meditations for Healing Stress audiotape is also good. It has music by Steven Halpern that is absolutely wonderful. Belleruth Naparstek has developed a variety of different meditations for particular health problems. I have used her Meditation for Successful Surgery with patients before surgery and had incredible success. You can find her tapes at www.healthjourneys.com. Finally, Shakti Gawain's Meditations audiotapes take you through four different meditations and are extraordinary.

You can also listen to soothing music of your choice— whatever works for you. The goal is to quiet your mind for brief periods, and when you do, magic occurs in your life.

One final note: when you begin to meditate, you may notice that a lot of old stuff comes to the surface. You are clearing your mind of the junk you have accumulated over the years. You are being asked to look at some of the old stuff and evaluate how your life was affected by past events. When this happens, look at the events from your past and consider how your life changed because of them. Also, look at what changes you have made in your life because of these events. Even though this can be unpleasant, it provides an opportunity to look at what has made you the person you are.

Deep breathing and meditation on a regular basis will release the tension in your body and fill you with the peace and joy you were meant to feel. Start today.

EXERCISES

Find a comfortable chair or go to your comfort spot. Relax, close your eyes, and place your hands on your belly. Breathe in through your nose and out through your mouth. Can you feel your muscles relax and the tension leave your body?

Do ten deep breaths every day for a week. Write how it feels on Day 1 and then on Day 7.

Pay attention to your breathing when you are stressed. If you are breathing shallowly, take a deep breath or two. Write about how it feels.

Try using the "I have all the time I need" and deep-breathing technique when you have ten things to do and only time to accomplish five. Write about what happens.

When you are in a stressful group situation, breathe in and out silently through your nose. Write about how this feels.

Meditate for five to ten minutes each morning for a week. Write out your list of intentions in a journal and read them before you meditate. The following week, increase your meditation time to fifteen minutes each day, then the next week increase it to twenty minutes each day. You will notice that this will give you extra energy throughout the day. When you are ready, add a late afternoon or early evening meditation in addition to your morning meditation. At the end of each week write about how you feel.

Journal about some of the past issues that come to you as you meditate.

♡

Breathing in, I calm myself
Breathing out, I feel at ease
Breathing in, I smile
Breathing out, I release
Breathing in,
I dwell in the present moment
Breathing out,
I feel it is a wonderful moment

Thich Nhat Hanh

FIVE

What do You Love to Do?

♡

What do you love to do? Few women can answer this question because they are used to taking care of others and not paying attention to their own needs. Most women do what their children or husbands want. They are the family's social director, so they spend much time making things happen for the family—and not for themselves.

What is it that you love to do? It is an important question. To find the answer you must be quiet and look inside. This can be done during your time of solitude in your comfort spot. You will discover that when you meditate, breathe, and relax, inspiration occurs and you will discover the answer.

As I was writing this chapter, I asked my daughter what she liked to do. Without hesitation she said, "I like to bake." She does love to bake and she is very good at it. It is something she has done since she was a young child. My medical assistant loves to make glass beads, and she is a natural at it. The joy she feels when she makes beads is evident. Think about what you enjoy doing and what you are good at. When you do what you love, you will feel joy.

Before you discover what you love to do, you might have to write down what you don't like to do. It can be an eye-opening experience when you realize you do a lot of things you don't like. For example, you may realize you don't have fun going to the beach. You don't like getting sandy and you don't enjoy going in the lake water because it has stuff in it. You do, however, enjoy being outside in the sun near water—but not on a sandy beach. You realize you like being at the pool, where the water is clean and there is no sand. Eureka! You know what you want. How can you make this happen?

Maybe there is something that sounds interesting to you, but you haven't tried it, so you don't know if you like it or not. Talk with people and listen to them. What have they done that sounds interesting? Take a class or join a group. Look through craft magazines. Visit the library. There is a whole world of fun things to do. Open your eyes and ears—discover what looks enjoyable to you.

As you begin doing what you love, you will be filled with joy. Sometimes it takes a while to get started. You may have to schedule time for your activity—that's okay. Push yourself to do it. After a couple of weeks you will start to move towards what you love with ease. A word of warning: once you begin doing what you love on a regular basis, it is ill advised to stop doing it. If you stop, your inner self will become irritable and your frustration will be shown in a variety of ways, none of them pretty. It is time to honor yourself and take time to do the things you love. When you do what you love, the joy you feel will spill onto the loved ones around you.

EXERCISES

One way to figure out what you like to do is by making a collage. Begin by gathering magazines and catalogues, then browse through them and cut out any photos that catch your eye. Don't analyze why something interests you, just cut it out. Paste the clippings into a collage. What do you see? Put the collage in a safe place and in a couple of days make another one. What is displayed in this collage? Do this exercise every few days. Is there a common theme to the photos? If so, your subconscious is telling you what you want.

Make a list of twenty things you like to do or would like to try doing. Take a few days to do this—or just sit down and see what comes to mind.

Go back and review your collages. Are there common activities that are on your list of twenty things you like to do? Can you add something to your list? Is there an activity that shows up in your collages several times that seems like a wild and crazy idea, something not really possible in your life at this time? If so, put it at the top of your list and dream about how you can make it a reality.

Prioritize your list. Pick your first, second, and third choices. Rewrite them in the format of "I intend to . . ."

Write down ten steps you will take towards reaching your top three choices. Take at least one step each week, and more if you like.

Choice One: I intend to _____

Choice Two: I intend to _____

Choice Three: I intend to _____

When you are ready to do what you love, schedule time for it each week. Write it on your calendar, in ink. Post a sign in your bathroom: "I am doing _____ every week" and do it. Write it here:

I am doing _____ every week.

Write down how it feels to do something that brings you joy on a regular basis. Can you do what you love more than once a week? How are you and your life changing because you are doing something that brings you joy? Write about it.

Dreams pass into the reality of action. From the action stems the dream again, and this interdependence produces the highest form of living.

Anais Nin

Six

What is Important to You?

$\heartsuit$

Do you rate yourself as being important—or do you think your family, friends, job, household chores, etc. have more priority than your needs? If you rate yourself lower than other people and your responsibilities, you need to think differently and take care of yourself.

This is not selfishness; it is self-preservation. If you don't take care of you—no one else will either—and eventually you will be no good to anyone. Keep in mind, usually when people call you selfish, they are saying this because they want you to do something for them. Or it may be that they have been so conditioned to never care for themselves they expect others to do the same.

How many tasks do you try to accomplish in one day? Do you want to do it all? If so, you are probably stressed and overwhelmed on a daily basis.

There is a solution. As my brother once reminded me, there are only twenty-four hours in a day, and some of those hours are spent sleeping, eating, and taking care of one's personal needs. He said, "You only have time for so much. What do you want to spend your time on?"

"I want to do it all," was my quick response.

"You can't," came his blunt reply.

His answer did not please me. Eventually, though, I realized if I tried to do it all, I was not doing my best at anything. I was too scattered. I also knew that those things that were important to me filled me up when I did them. The activities that weren't important to me drained me; so I had even less time and energy for what was important.

It is imperative that you take care of your body, mind, and spirit. Your physical health must be a top priority. To function and do the things you want, your body must be well cared for. When your body speaks to you, it is your intuition, your Truth. Your mind may try to downplay your intuition, and that often leads to trouble. Your body cannot speak to you if it is not being taken care of.

It is important to feed your mind positive and uplifting information. And your spirit will feed your heart and soul when you allow joy and light into your life.

To determine if you are spending your time and energy on that which is important to you, reflect on various aspects of your life. What people and relationships are important to you? Who makes you feel good about yourself? People that make you feel bad drain your energy. Do you want to continue to lose energy to someone who gives nothing back or would you rather put your time towards people who make you feel good and build up your energy?

How much time do you spend with your children? Children

need to be with their parents, rather than shuffled from one activity to another. Your children want to be with you. That is how they learn about life.

How much time do you spend with your significant other? One of the reasons the divorce rate is so high is that couples do not spend enough time on their relationships. Marriages are shoved onto back burners and expected to survive. But they can't. Nothing survives if it isn't taken care of. Spending just ten minutes per day talking with your significant other can help you connect again, and going out on a date once a week is also important.

How about your friendships? A wise sixty-five-year-old woman in the Soul Comfort class said, "You only have three or four really good friends in a lifetime, the rest are just acquaintances." Are you spending more time with your acquaintances than you are with your true friends?

Finally, what do you love to do? (You should have answered this question in Chapter 5.) What makes you get out of bed in the morning, other than the million and one things you have on your to-do list? What brings you pleasure? Your health and relationships are important, but you also need to take time to do what you love to do. The joy you feel when doing what you love will affect your health and relationships.

Spending time on what is important to you—and not others—can be a challenge. But the bliss you will find when you focus on what is important to you is beyond compare.

EXERCISES

What is important to you? List only three or four things, activities, or people.

Write down the things, activities, or people you can let go of at this time. When they come back into your life, and they most likely will, you can release them again and fill up with what is truly important to you.

Remember the Five Ps: Prior Proper Planning Prevents Problems. How much time are you going to spend on your health? What are you going to do to get and stay healthy? Write out your plan.

How much time are you going to spend with your significant other every day? Each week? Seek input from your significant other and write down a plan. Write about how it feels to spend time with your significant other.

If you are not in a committed relationship, spend more time getting to know yourself. Go back and review Chapter 2. Write about how you are spending your time in solitude and how it feels. If you are spending more time with friends, write about how that feels.

Write out a plan for spending one-on-one time with each of your children. Ask for their input. How can you do this on a regular basis? Write about how it feels to spend time with your kids. If you don't have children, can you spend time with your nieces and nephews? Is there a child in the community you can mentor? Get involved with Big Brothers/Big Sisters. You can have incredible impact on children when you spend time with them. Write about the children you spend time with and how it feels.

Write down your top three choices from Chapter 5. Are you making time for these activities? As you begin to release those people and things that are not your top priorities, you will find the time to do what you love, and this will fill you with joy.

Putting first things first means organizing and executing your most important priorities. It is living and being driven by the principles you value most, not by the agendas and forces surrounding you.

Stephen R. Covey

SEVEN

Feeling Stuffers

How are you doing? Are you letting your light shine? If you find it difficult to feel joy, you are not alone. Everyone has "joy snatchers" in their lives. Sometimes, no matter how hard you try to find your joy, you realize you can't overcome the joy snatchers. To defeat the joy snatchers, you have to face them head-on, work through them, and then release them. When you do this, you will free up space to allow more joy into your life.

Let us begin by looking at the first joy snatcher: feeling stuffers. Feeling stuffers are actions or substances that you use to not feel. In other words, they are addictions. You are using a feeling stuffer when you say "I deserve this" and then you enjoy whatever "this" is while you are doing it, but later wish you hadn't.

There is a gamut of things people do to avoid feeling, such

as eating, smoking, drinking, gambling, taking prescription and nonprescription drugs, sex, shopping, taking care of the world, working, etc. The difference between a feeling stuffer and a pleasurable activity—which most of these things can be—is how you feel after you have imbibed.

For example, you can go out with friends and have a couple of cocktails. When you get home you are smiling because of the fun you had, and the next day you feel great. Or you can go out with friends with the intention of having a couple of cocktails. However, you forget to stop after two drinks and get drunk. When you wake up the next morning, you feel awful from the hangover and because you don't remember everything that happened the night before. That is a feeling stuffer.

Another example is shopping. You go shopping for the day, purchase a couple of items on sale, and have a wonderful excursion—compared to spending all of your cash and maxing out your credit cards on things you don't need. Now you hope there is enough money in your checking account for groceries this week. That is a feeling stuffer.

Feeling stuffers may be the only "pleasure" you get on a regular basis—a box of cookies, a pack of cigarettes, a bottle of wine—because there is no time for anything else that you enjoy. You don't even know what you like to do because you have too many things to do for everyone else.

Feeling stuffers will give you pleasure in the moment—but cause you pain later on.

Why else do you do this? Life can be pretty tough and many women are in situations that do not fill them with joy. It is much easier to shut down than to wake up and say, "I need to make some changes." You do anything to avoid feeling. When you feel too much it can be painful and scary; and you might realize you have to make some changes in your life.

I am seeing this behavior more and more in my practice and it concerns me greatly. The complaint comes in two forms. The first one is: "I am anxious, depressed or think I am bipolar and need medication." The other complaint is: "The medicine is not working." I believe in the use of medication. I have seen patients with a lifelong history of anxiety, depression, or bipolar disease change dramatically with the use of medication. They are living full lives for the first time. I am not talking about this group of people.

I am talking about women who feel their emotions are out of control. They yell at their kids or their husband or the dog. They feel guilty, try to make up for it, promise never to do it again and then it happens again, and the cycle repeats itself. They have used a variety of over-the-counter feeling stuffers and are now looking for medication to stop those feelings. Their emotions are a reaction to the insanity of their lives. But they are told they are wrong to react, to feel like this, and their emotions must be stopped so the insanity can continue.

I say No! Women are emotional creatures; our hormones make us that way. It is what makes us different than men. What we need to do is stop using feeling stuffers and look at what is underneath that rage and begin to fix what is causing the anger, not stuff it down even deeper.

Let me give you an example. A patient, whom I had not seen for months, came in with her husband. She was requesting medication for bipolar disease that was recently diagnosed by a psychologist. I had known this woman a long time, and even though I am a nurse practitioner and not a psychologist I was not convinced she was bipolar. Her primary complaint was she felt out of control at home, i.e., yelled at her husband and children—but she was fine at work. The psychologist told her she was cycling rapidly. I said it sounded like a situational problem to me. She had been through an incredible number of changes over the last couple of years and her two children were under the age of four. I told her she was just speaking (yelling) the emotions of her family and that this was normal. I asked if she had talked with her sisters about her home life. No, she hadn't because she felt so bad about it. Things were finally starting to level out in her life, and she could see good things coming, but she was still yelling.

I suggested we wait on the medication, she should spend some alone time with her husband, stop feeling guilty about not being super mom with the kids, talk with her sisters, go have fun with her sisters and friends, and get back to me in a month or sooner if needed. She came bouncing back in a month later with a big smile on her face. She had talked to her sisters and realized she was just fine, thank you very much. The changes had sorted themselves out and she knew she and her family would be fine.

Take time to look at the cause of your feelings before you try to run from them with feeling stuffers. Talk to someone about how you can release the negative feelings and emotions instead of stuff them.

How do you give up your feeling stuffers, your addictions? First, you must decide that you want to make changes in your life. The next step is to ask yourself what you can do differently. What can you do that will fill you up rather than hurt you?

Many women don't have a clue because they have used feeling stuffers for too long. Maybe your inner voice is so used to being ignored, it has stopped talking. Or you may find that when your inner voice speaks, you say, "I can't do that." For example, it says, "I need a nap". But you stifle the suggestion with" "There are a million things I have to do; I do not have time for a nap." So, you reach for a cookie to keep you going.

Unfortunately, in an hour you will probably be more tired and still have a million things to do. If you had rested for fifteen minutes you would have felt energized and accomplished at least a couple of the things on your long list.

It takes time and practice to listen to your inner voice. It takes time to honor yourself—but once you do, life becomes truly pleasurable. When you take time to fulfill your needs, your inner self says, "Thank you." Then you will feel joy.

When you start to crave your favorite feeling stuffer, take a moment to gently ask yourself, "How can I nurture myself?" Take a deep breath, listen, and then follow through with what your inner voice tells you. The more you do this, the more joy you get. That is what life is about.

How can you nurture yourself? What can you do differently? Go back to Chapters 5 and 6. Instead of using a feeling stuffer, perhaps you can do something you love to do. Try it and you will be amazed at how doing something you love will fill you up and you won't need that feeling stuffer.

When was the last time you did what was important to you? If it has been a while, if you have been giving all your energy to people and activities that aren't important to you, you will be having strong urges for a feeling stuffer. Why? Because your inner self is getting tired of taking care of the world and not you. And the quickest way to quiet your inner self is to reach for a feeling stuffer.

Another suggestion is to remove feeling stuffers from your home, i.e., sugar, cigarettes, alcohol, catalogues, etc. They will call your name if they are present.

In a moment of weakness, you may end up driving to the store to get a favorite feeling stuffer, but that's okay. Eventually, before grabbing the car keys to satisfy your urgent "need," you will ask: "How can I nurture myself? What can I do differently?" In time you will automatically go for the healthier alternative.

One final question: do you have to be good all the time? Can you splurge and have something sweet, a cigarette, a drink, go shopping, or gambling? You can, if you choose—but know that there will be consequences. My personal feeling stuffer is sugar, to which my body reacts strongly. I find that when I eat sugar not only do I feel terrible that day but also the next day. Most of the time when I crave sugar, I can ask myself if it is worth feeling bad today and tomorrow. Sometimes I say yes; but most often I can ask myself "What can I do to nurture myself?" and then I do it.

When you first stop using feeling stuffers you may feel pain. But don't give in to the desire. Soon enough you will experience joy because you didn't succumb to shutting down your feelings.

This is how you add more joy to your life—by acknowledging your feelings and taking action to make the changes in your life that need to be made. As you resolve these issues you won't need feeling stuffers.

It is an ongoing process of looking at how you feel and how you want to feel, and making the changes that need to be made.

EXERCISES

How do you stuff your feelings? What is your addiction(s)? Take some time to consider your answer. Usually women have a significant feeling stuffer and several smaller ones. How do these behaviors/addictions make you feel? Write down your answers.

Look at your life. Are you and your family living a chaotic insane environment? Are your emotions simply the feminine voice of the insane lifestyle that you are living? Who can you talk with to help you sort this out? How can you nurture yourself and begin to move away from the chaos and insanity toward more joy and pleasure?

How can you nurture yourself instead of eating those cookies, smoking that cigarette, or drinking a glass of wine? Go back to Chapters 5 and 6. Write down the people and activities that are important to you. These will be positive alternatives to feeling stuffers.

What feelings are you avoiding? Is it anger, despair, loneliness, guilt, frustration? Instead of avoiding your feelings, journal about them, call a friend, and/or seek professional counseling.

Describe in words or pictorially the feelings that you most often try to avoid.

♡

Addiction is the disease of our age. It is cunning and powerful . . . Addiction grows fat from our chronic squashing of the inner life.

Erica Jong

Eight

Human Beings

Women are human *beings* not human *doings*. Yet we are always on the run. Busy, busy, busy. "No time to say hello, good-bye. I'm late, I'm late, I'm late!" says the rabbit in *Alice in Wonderland*.

Who told us we are always supposed to be doing something? Why do we believe we shouldn't rest unless we are recuperating from an accident or illness? Why do we keep up with the insanity of having our schedules so full that we have no time to breathe?

When was the last time you sat in a chair and did nothing— for even just a few minutes? When was the last time you practiced the art of being? This *is* an art and it takes practice because women are used to *doing* instead of *being*.

What does *being* mean? It means to sit and not think or do anything, which can be difficult. Women are trained to always be doing something, until they collapse at the end of the day from exhaustion. Exhaustion is a numbness that shuts down your essence. Being allows your essence to shine.

There may be times when you sit down for a moment—but how often does your mind go to the past or the future—instead of just being in the moment? How often does your mind race with "I need to do this," "I need to do that," "I can't believe that happened," etc.? How often do you look around a room and see everything that needs to be done instead of enjoying the things that are done? When was the last time you sat outdoors for a moment and enjoyed the beauty of nature?

Your body requires this art of being. Your body needs to rest while you are awake, instead of being pushed to its limits until you collapse. If you treated your car as poorly as you treat yourself, it would only last a couple of years.

It is time to stop doing. Rip the S for Superwoman off the front of your shirt, and practice being. This will be difficult, but in time you will enjoy the wonderful feeling.

Find a moment each day when you can take a break. Find a comfortable chair or go to your comfort spot. You may need to alert your family to the fact that you are just going to *be* for a while and do not want to be disturbed. This may require setting a timer and going behind closed doors. That's okay, do it. Once you are there, close your eyes and take a deep breath. Focus on the air coming into and going out of your lungs. Take another deep breath and focus on the air coming in and going out. Can you feel yourself starting to relax? Are the muscles in your shoulders losing their tension? Now, open your eyes and look at something that brings you pleasure. Avoid looking at the stuff that causes you distress. Let your mind wander; but if you feel yourself thinking hard about something, bring your mind back to the moment. Focus your attention on your heart center and feel the warmth flowing inside of you. Sit for as long as you can, then take a deep breath, rise slowly, and enter back into your human, doing life.

When you first do this, you will be met with a huge amount of resistance. The voice in your head, your inner critic, will tell you there is no time to just sit around. "Get going! Look at all the things in this room that need to be taken care of . . . !" Whose voice is that? Why is it so terrible to sit down and relax for a few moments?

At first, you may only be able to sit quietly for a minute or two. Keep practicing and eventually—it may be months or years—you will be able to do this for longer periods of time

An unknown author wrote "I have to rest my body so my spirit can catch up with me." Your body, mind, and spirit crave the state of being. When you have overworked your body and your mind is in frenzy, your spirit fades into nothingness. When your spirit is gone, there is no joy. When you rest your body and mind through the art of being, your spirit will return. When your spirit returns, you will feel joy again.

Are you ready to learn the art of being?

EXERCISES

Find a time and place where you can have at least a couple minutes of silence. Close your eyes and take a few deep breaths. Open your eyes, let your mind wander, and just be. Do this every day for one week. Journal how it feels each day. Did it get easier by the end of the week?

Soothe your inner critic with a thank you for its opinion. Tell it that you are just going to be here for a little while, then you will get back to work. Write about how it feels to quiet your inner critic.

Too many people, too many demands,
too much to do; busy hurrying people.
It just isn't living at all.

Anne Morrow Lindbergh

NINE

Television

Watching television is one of the greatest joy snatchers of all because it is a huge waste of time and it promotes depression. The A.C. Nielsen Co. reports that the average American watches more than four hours of TV daily. This is equal to two months of non-stop television viewing per year. By the time you reach age sixty-five you have spent nine years in front of the TV (www.csun.edu). Think about it, four hours a day and nine years in a lifetime.

Watching TV can be as addictive as any bad habit. In *Four Arguments for the Elimination of Television*, Jerry Mander says that TV hypnotizes people. Watch anyone who is focused on a program. They are completely zoned out to anything else around them. He writes: "Imagining a world free of television, I can only imagine beneficial effects . . . Chances are excellent that human beings, once outside the cloud of television images would be happier than they have been of late, once again living in a reality which is less artificial, less imposed, and more responsive to personal action."

The most common complaint I hear from people is that they never have enough time. If you turned off the TV, how much extra time would you have each day? How would you feel? How would your life begin to change?

Television has also contributed to the obesity problem in America. Do you eat while you watch TV? All those commercials can certainly make you think you are hungry.

And, watching the news and crime programs on a daily basis can be depressing—and stressful. I have had several patients say they cry a lot when they watch the news. I told them to stop watching the news and let me know what happens. Many reported feeling much better. If you find that you compulsively watch programs that cause you stress, take a break. You may be surprised at the difference. Life is hard enough and there is no reason to immerse yourself into seemingly nonstop violence, sadness, grief, etc.

Does this mean you should not help others? Absolutely not! Sending prayers, money, clothing, food, and other support to causes you strongly believe in is good for your soul. Taking action in the face of tragedy is healing; ranting and raving about something that has already happened does no one any good.

There are, however, some educational programs available, i.e., home improvement, gardening, crafts, decorating. These can be helpful in helping you meet a goal, which is a good thing.

If you want joy in your life and are a chronic TV viewer you will have to make some changes in your life. Are you ready to set aside the remote?

EXERCISES

Monitor your TV viewing for one week and write down how much time you spent watching it. Also write down the programs you watched and how much time was spent flipping through the channels.

Evaluate what you watch. How much time was spent viewing the news compared to educational programs? Write down how you felt after watching each type of program.

Next, stop watching TV for one week. But, before you begin this, make a list of things that you have always wanted to do and never had time for. Review your lists from previous chapters. You can also use this free time to hang out in your comfort spot. Have fun!! Each day write down what you did instead of watch TV and how it feels.

How much time do you want to devote to watching television versus inviting joy into your life? After a week of no television, go back and read what you wrote when you monitored and evaluated your TV intake. Are there any shows you want to add back into your life? What programs will you now avoid? Write down activities you can do to replace watching these shows. How many movies do you want to watch each week? Write down how much time this will consume. Make notes to remind yourself to not turn on the TV out of boredom. Good luck—you can do this.

I find television very educating.
Every time someone turns on the set,
I go into the other room
and read a good book.

Groucho Marx

TEN

Creativity and Healing

If you believe you don't have a creative bone in your body, read on. This chapter may help you get over your creativity block.

Being creative fills your soul in a way nothing else can. Generations ago, women were creative all day. They cooked, baked, quilted, weaved, sewed, etc. Today, women don't have to create so much because most products can be purchased ready-made. Although this convenience saves us time and energy, what we have lost is the meditative activity of creating.

When you sew, knit, quilt, bake, etc., you work in a rhythmic manner that gives your mind time to slow down, to wander, and to contemplate. Even though it was necessary work, women were able to find peace and tranquility in these hands-on activities. In today's hectic, crazy world, women need creative time more than ever.

Creativity is healing. For example, when a loved one dies, make a project in his or her honor, something to express your love and grief. I recently recommended this to a patient whose mother had died. She decided to make a quilt out of all the housecoats and nightgowns her mother used to wear. What a heart-warming idea.

Other creative ways to heal from grief are: making a photo album, writing your memories about the person, planting a garden, building a birdhouse, etc. Time heals all wounds and doing something creative helps you get through that time a little easier.

Losing a loved one is not the only loss that can be helped with a creative endeavor. Going through a divorce, not getting a job you wanted, sending a child off to college, having a friend move away—all require a period of time to heal. With any loss there occurs an empty space in your being. You can fill the void with anger, depression, rage, anxiety, fear, hopelessness, and other negative emotions—or you can use your creativity to heal in a positive manner and avoid falling back on feeling stuffers.

Creativity allows you to feel pride in yourself—for completing something tangible. Don't strive for perfection; rather bask in the healing grace of doing something to completion.

Perfectionism takes the joy out of life fully and completely. One technique to get rid of any perfectionist qualities you have is to step outside yourself. Then, look at your project as if your dearest friend or child made it. How would you accept the gift? Are you going to point out its faults or acknowledge its beauty and originality? Give yourself this same consideration. It feels good when you are nice to yourself.

Feel the joy that comes with a job well done. Hear and feel the compliments that people pay you. I remember a patient telling me she had painted Christmas cards and mailed them to her friends and family. She received a phone call from a family member raving about the cards and wondering where she purchased them. My patient said, "I painted them." To which the family member immediately said, "You are an incredible painter!" I could see the joy, pride, and a bit of disbelief in my patient's eyes. Release that disbelief as others compliment you. Let go of the thought: "Oh, they are just saying that to be nice." No, they aren't. They really mean it.

Listen to their voices. Let the words of praise fill you up with the joy they were intended to give.

Pay attention to the joy you feel as you release your creative self.

EXERCISES

What can you do that is creative? Make a list of the items you will need for the project—then go out and purchase them.

When will you be creative? Commit to at least twice per week. Write down when you will be creative; then write it in your planner, in ink.

If nothing comes to mind, start collecting magazines and make a collage of activities/projects that are appealing. Do this for two weeks. What shows up? Write about it.

If you want to learn a new craft, who will teach you? Is there a class you can take in your community or a friend or family member that can teach you? Check it out and write about whom will help you learn your new activity.

If you have experienced a loss, think about a project you can do to help you grieve and heal. If a loved one has died, dedicate a project to that person. If you lost a job, are going through a divorce, or have had some other loss, dedicate a project to yourself and the new person you will be as you emerge from this loss. Write about the project, i.e., to whom you will dedicate it and when you will do it. Then, begin.

When you have completed your project, show it to someone who loves and supports you fully. Do not, I repeat, do NOT show it to someone who will criticize your work. This could send your creative being so far within you; it will be a long time before you see her again. Ask the person you trust what she thinks. Feel the praise and joy her words bring to you. Write about how you feel and how proud you are of yourself for your accomplishment.

What's your next project?

Creativity can solve almost any problem.
The creative act, the defeat of habit
by originality, overcomes everything.

George Lois

ELEVEN

Relationships

What are your relationships like? Do you have good relationships or do most of them fall into the category of joy snatchers? A good relationship is with someone that makes you feel wonderful, someone that adds joy to your life. When you think about being with him or her and when you are with him or her, you feel excitement. It is someone that brightens your day.

A bad relationship is the opposite. It is one that makes you feel terrible when you are with that person or even think about being with that person. Do you know someone that brings you down? Pay attention to how your body feels and where you feel it. Do you get a sinking sensation in your gut? Do you get a headache? Does your back start to get tense and hurt?

Now, think about a pleasant relationship. What and how do you feel? Do you get a flicker of joy in your chest? Does your heart beat faster? Does a smile form? This is how you should feel when you are with friends and family.

The awful feelings described above are not what you want in your life on a continual basis because eventually you will get sick. What goes on in your mind and what you feel affects your physical health. When you are surrounded by bad relationships you will get sick.

As you get older, you become wiser and your body speaks louder when your self is not being honored. This shows up in frequent illnesses and various diseases. How does your body speak to you when you are around people who make you feel bad?

Recently, a patient came in with laryngitis. I prescribed some herbs and teas to help her heal, and then I suggested that something in her life was causing her not to speak. "Have you had any changes or increased stress lately?" I asked. She said, "My mother-in-law has been at my home for the last four days and won't be leaving for three more days." We both laughed, then we discussed some strategies to help her get through the next few days and any future visits by her mother-in-law.

A more extreme example of mind/body medicine is a patient who experienced incredible abdominal pain whenever her father phoned. She was terribly abused by him as a child —but she thought she should be nice to him because he is her father.

She would be in my office for a checkup and be fine. The next week, however, she would come in with incredible pain in her entire abdominal region. I would ask her what happened and eventually she would reveal that her father had called and wanted her to do something for him.

I ordered a multitude of tests to make sure nothing was physically wrong—they came back normal. But her symptoms were not just in her head. She was physically ill. Her gut was screaming: "I can not be in this relationship with my father."

Fortunately, over the last year, with support from her counselor, her incredibly loving fiancé, and our office, she has made the decision to not accept her father's phone calls. She still has her ups and downs—but for the most part she is doing great and her abdominal pain has ceased.

Why do we stay in toxic relationships? Why do we allow people that make us miserable or physically ill into our lives? Why do we let some relationships snatch the joy out of our lives? Sometimes it's because it seems like the right thing to do, i.e., "I'm doing it for the kids" or "I need this job." In the book *Illusions, the Adventure of the Reluctant Messiah*, Richard Bach writes: "The bond that links your true family is not one of blood, but of respect and joy in each other's life. Rarely do members of one family grow up under the same roof."

Think about the last time you were with your family. Were you treated with respect? Did you feel joy? If not, it is time to make some changes.

One of my patients has seasonal affective disorder (SAD). I told her she needed to make some changes in her life because each year she gets worse. I suggested she move to a sunny climate. "I can't," she replied. "I have to take care of my family." I told her that her family was killing her, even though I know them and know they love her. Whenever anyone needs this woman, she drops everything and runs to fix the problem. She is addicted to caregiving and it is killing her.

Two weeks later, in a follow-up visit, she said she was setting boundaries and making changes. I could already see the difference in her—even though the sun had not been shining.

It is hard for this woman to be "selfish," as her family sometimes calls her. I tell her she is not being selfish; it is self-preservation. "You are no good to anyone if you are completely empty of any life-giving force. You have to take care of yourself and the joy you feel will reflect on those around you. That is all you can do," I said.

When I hear women say they can't leave a toxic marriage because of the children I wonder what they are teaching their children about marriage. Are they teaching daughters that it is all right to be verbally abused by a husband or treated as a personal assistant? Are they teaching sons that women do not deserve love and respect? Children watch their parents and will repeat their behaviors when they, too, become adults.

Don't let the fear of loneliness stop you from making alterations that will better your health and allow joy into your life. Yes, there are lonely moments when you are first divorced, but those moments can be less lonely than what you experienced in the marriage. I remember talking to a friend a few years after her divorce. She said, "I knew I had to leave because there had to be something better than this." I saw her last week and almost didn't recognize her. She remarried last summer, lost a lot of weight, and was glowing. What a joy she was to see.

The goal is to be able to answer yes to Oriah Mountain Dreamer's question in her book *The Invitation*. She asks: "I want to know if you can be alone with yourself and if you truly like the company you keep in the empty moments." Sadly, most people have never had any time alone. Many people prefer not to be alone and will do anything to prevent spending time by themselves. Being alone is not always easy, but it is the only way to make changes in your life. You need to take quiet time to look at your life and reflect on where you've been, where you are, and where you want to go.

Am I a proponent of divorce? At times, yes. If the marriage is only causing misery, it is time to move on. However, many of my patients who are unhappily married love their spouses, but simply have not put time into making the relationships work. With these women, I ask them to think back to what made them fall in love with their husbands. What did they do together then? What can they enjoy doing together now? When was the last time they went out on a date or went away together? By simply spending time together, the relationship can improve. Which is true about anything. If you don't put time or effort into something, it will die.

For others, though, the marriage died a long time ago and there is no hope for revival. The sadness I see in these women is heartbreaking. They decide to stay in the marriage because they don't want to hurt their husbands or their children. What they are doing is slowly killing themselves. They are preventing themselves—and their spouses—from moving on and being in a loving relationship. Oftentimes in these marriages, there have been years of neglect and abuse. This loss of hope manifests itself in several ways. It may be anger and rage directed at a spouse on a daily basis—or withdrawal and silence. Either one is not the way to live.

Basically, the love the woman felt for her husband has been destroyed and there is no hope of reviving it, no matter what he does. When love and appreciation are nonexistent in a marriage, one's spirit starts to die. Once all hope has been lost, divorce may not be inevitable, but the pain, rage, and despair will continue until you get out of the relationship.

Is it easy to leave a relationship? No. Is it easy after you have left the relationship? At times, yes; other times, no.

It is important to make an effort to make your marriage work. I recommend counseling for people who are struggling in their relationships. Professional counseling can clarify what it is that you need and how you can get those needs met in the relationship. If you cannot get your needs met, it is time to go. Life is too short to remain in a miserable relationship. Life is meant to be enjoyed.

Pay attention to your body; it doesn't lie; though your mind can. Your mind will say: "I am fine, just fine, thank you." In the meantime, your body is sending you signals that things are not okay. When your body starts talking to you, pay attention and ask yourself these questions:

- Do I feel joy with this person?
- Do I wake up happy?
- What are my hopes and dreams? Are they mine or his?
- Are we a spiritual match?
- What do my friends think of him? (They know.)
- Do I like people or am I full of judgment?
- How am I with my child(ren)?
- How am I with my friends?
- Am I being true to my Self?
- Am I answering the above questions truthfully, from my heart?
- How am I at work?
- Do I laugh?
- Am I having fun?
- Do I exercise and eat healthy?
- Have I increased my use of feeling stuffers?
- Am I doing what I like to do?
- What am I giving up that I can live without?
- Once again, am I being true to my Self?

If you answer any of the above questions with a no, and they were yes before you entered the relationship, it is time to rethink the relationship. Will everything be perfect in a relationship? Absolutely not. We learn our most valuable lessons by being in relationships with people. And, ironically, it is usually the difficult ones that we learn from the most.

I would also ask you to take a look at how your body is feeling. Are you having more migraines, irritable bowel attacks, stomachaches, fatigue, back or neck pain, colds or sinus infections, heavier periods, irregular bleeding, more hot flashes or night sweats? Are you using more feeling stuffers? How is your body speaking to you as you are in this relationship? Your body can be a true indicator of how your life is going. Pay attention.

If you are not receiving the love and respect you deserve, it is time to establish different relationships. Think about what interests you and seek like-minded people. Consider joining a different community organization or volunteering.

Work can also bring difficult relationships into your life. Do you like your job? Do you like the people you work with? Is there anything good about your job or do you hate it absolutely and completely? If you hate your job absolutely and completely it is time to find a new one. If you feel you are stuck in a job because of finances or other responsibilities, then it is time to think about how you can find a different one. It may take a year, or several years, but make an effort to change the situation that you hate.

If there are aspects of your job that you like, focus on those and think of ways to improve your job even more. When your mind starts to wander toward the negative aspects, bring it back to the positive. Then, see how you feel after you've practiced this technique for a while on a regular basis.

Pay attention to how you feel with your friends. Do they energize you or bring you down? Do not waste your precious life and lose your joy by spending time with people who depress you. Move away from the negative friendships and find friends that bring you joy.

You may be going through a period when few people bring you joy. This is when you need to spend time in solitude to evaluate what you want in life. You should ask yourself the questions Howard Thurman asks: "Where am I going?" and "Who will go with me?" (These questions should not be asked in the reverse order.)

This can be a lonely time; but as you work through it, you will attract people who will bring you joy.

EXERCISES

For one week, be aware of how you feel with the people you meet each day. Here and there take a moment to check in with your body when you are with a variety of people. The more you do this, the more clearly you will understand how your body talks to you. Write about a couple of good instances and bad instances that occurred during the week.

Spend time with a person you enjoy. Face-to-face interaction is preferred, but if it has to be with a phone call, that's okay. Write down how you felt before, during, and after your meeting.

Focus on how you feel when you are near someone that does not bring you joy. Where in your body do you feel something? Write about this person, how you feel, and where you experienced sensation in your body.

What can you do to change your reaction to this negative relationship? How much more time do you want to waste on feeling bad? When will you put your attention on those relationships that bring you joy? Write down one thing YOU can do that can change how YOU react to this person.

Define your job. What do you like about it? What don't you like about it? If you could do anything you love and not have to worry about being paid for it, what would you do? How can you bring that which you love to do into your life?

Focus on what you like about your job for one week. Write down at the end of each day how you feel.

Look at your friendships. Write about one friend that makes you feel good and one friend that makes you feel bad. How can you move towards the friendship that brings you joy and move away from the friendship that brings you despair? Remember the twenty-four-hour rule. If you spend more time with the friends that bring you joy, there will be less time to spend with those that bring you despair. Write about how you can spend more time with the friends that bring you joy. If you discover that few of your friendships bring you joy, go back to Chapter 2. Re-read it and spend time in solitude. Then, write about what kind of friend you would like to have. Believe this person can come into your life and watch for the opportunities that will present themselves to you.

The quality of your life is the quality of your relationships.

Anthony Robbins

TWELVE

Family and Friends

When was the last time you saw friends and family members that bring you joy? If it has been a while, bring these people back into your life.

When was the last time you took off for a girl's weekend? A sisters' weekend? Never? You are missing out. It is time to talk with the women in your life and schedule a weekend without children or spouses. It doesn't have to be far away or expensive. The goal is to get away from all responsibility, and to laugh, eat, and have fun.

For many women, the older they get the more they desire female companionship. I think this happens because women want to be around people who think like they do. There is comfort in realizing you are not going crazy—that others feel the same way.

If a weekend away sounds impossible, then start with a lunch date. How many times have you said to someone, "Let's get together for lunch" and it never happens? Today is the day to do it. Think about whom you want to visit with and make the phone call(s). If lunch doesn't work, then make it a dinner date.

Some women meet as a group once a month. They go to dinner, to the movies, discuss books, play cards . . . whatever. The point is—they have fun without children or husbands.

The Red Hat Ladies is becoming a popular group to join. Whenever I see these women it looks like they are having a good time. You may want to start such a group. Think about what you would like to do—then ask other women to join you.

Who in your family brings you joy? Who in your family would you like to get to know better? Are there distant relatives you would like to make contact with? When was the last time you saw your grandparents or your aunts and uncles? Can you begin a new relationship with them? Call or write to them today. Family can be an important connection in life.

EXERCISES

Ask someone out for lunch or dinner this week. It can be an old friend or someone you might like to get to know better. Write about how the meeting went and how you felt. Make plans to meet with the same person or someone else in the next couple of weeks.

How did the second date go? Was it with the same person or someone new? Continue this pattern on a regular basis. Get together with a friend, new or old, every week or two. Write about what you do. Write about how you feel before, after, and during your time together.

How about starting a group? Meet with a friend or two and brainstorm about what type of activity you want the group to do on a monthly basis. Then, contact other women and schedule the first meeting. Write the meeting date in ink in your planner. Write about what the group will do, who will be in it, and when you will meet. Be creative.

Who in your family brings you joy? Who would you like to get to know better in your family? Call them and set a time to meet—or just talk with them on the phone. E-mail can also be a way to connect with people on a regular basis.

Do you have a yearly family reunion? If not, find a relative and plan one. Begin having an annual family reunion. Write about how you feel about attending an annual family gathering. If this strikes terror in your heart, re-read Chapter 11. What you may choose to do instead is have an annual girlfriend reunion.

Sometimes our light goes out but is blown into flame by another human being. Each of us owes deepest thanks to those who have rekindled this light.

Albert Schweitzer

THIRTEEN

The Butterfly: Transformation

A butterfly's life cycle has four stages: it begins as a tiny egg, grows into a caterpillar, wraps itself into a cocoon, and then emerges as a butterfly. Immediately after breaking free of the cocoon, it rests for a while to get used to its new wings—before taking flight into a new way of being.

Women can look at the butterfly's life cycle to understand the transformation their lives also take. Like a caterpillar, we start as an egg; and, after birth, take in all that life offers us. Just as a caterpillar outgrows its skin five times before it enters the cocoon, our life experiences prepare us for our final stage of becoming a butterfly and living life differently. Many "old skins" will be shed as we mature.

Inside of its cocoon, a caterpillar melts down, dissolves into liquid, and then is finally transformed into a butterfly. Have you ever had a meltdown and exited the event a different person? That is part of life.

Meltdowns occur any number of times in a woman's life. They entail significant change, usually caused by outside events that let your inner self know something is wrong, i.e., "I need to do something because I can no longer live this way."

Transformations can be difficult, but they are imperative for keeping joy in your life. (Also of note, is that the cocoon is attached to something for support. As you go through major transformations, it's okay to reach out and ask for help. Without support you are like a leaf blowing in the wind. You will be unable to settle, to ground, to transform into something new.)

Realize, that any transformation you go through is completely normal and natural. Many women are or have had the same experience. It's a transition, and with time and help from others you will come out on the other side.

Having a meltdown is not a comfortable life experience, and some women get freaked out. "I don't want to be different. I like myself the way I am" or "I don't want to change. It's easier to keep things as they are." You have no choice. Just as the caterpillar, you must allow yourself to transform into a butterfly.

To prepare your cocoon, you must spend time in solitude (see Chapter 2). Allow the meltdown to occur and look forward to emerging as a new person. If you hurry or disregard this transition, you may miss the lesson or healing that can occur during this transformation.

For example, although anxiety and depression can be a part of the transformation, if you don't make the changes that are needed to transform, the depression and anxiety can linger. You may become bitter. You may slip into an addiction. You may eat more, smoke more, drink more, shop more, work more, etc. If you do this, you will shut down your heart energy and wonder why your life feels so empty. You may get sick or develop a disease.

How do you spin your cocoon? You first need to forgive yourself. You are not made of steel and everyone has melt-downs—it is how women change and grow. Then review Chapter 3 for ideas on finding a comfort spot. Spend time in your comfort spot; it is your cocoon. Next set boundaries— establish the walls of your cocoon. Without these your cocoon will crumble and your transformation will not be complete.

Again, seek the support of family or friends. Do you need a counselor or a spiritual director? Sometimes an objective opin-ion is beneficial. As one patient said, "I came to you because I knew my friends would say my husband is a jerk and I should leave him. I want you to help me look at this from a different perspective and give me hope."

How do you nourish your body, heart, and soul as you go through this transition? Feed your body wholesome foods. Comfort (snack) foods will only cause more anxiety and depression. What warms your heart? Is it your animals, being in nature, or listening to music? What can you listen to or read to soothe your soul? You may not be able to focus much, but a passage here and there can give you hope.

Do you need to cry? Watch a sad movie. Watch it again if you want. Everybody needs a good two-hour cry once in a while. Tears are healing. Release your tears instead of keeping them bottled up inside.

When you are in your cocoon, you will begin to transform into your new self. You will see a light at the end of the tunnel and know it is not a train coming at you. You will start to feel hope and know you will be all right. You will become a but-terfly and soon be ready to fly.

As the butterfly exits its cocoon, it must exert itself to get out. It's not an easy process. Once it emerges, it expands and strengthens its wings. If a human "helps" release a butterfly from its cocoon, so that it doesn't have to exert itself, the butterfly will be crippled for life. This is profound.

You, too, must exert yourself to become a new you. Nobody can do it for you. You have to set your boundaries and strengthen your wings before you can fly. You can have the support of others, as the cocoon is attached to the branch, but you must do the work yourself.

When you first emerge from your transformation, you are vulnerable. You may need the support and encouragement of others for a while. "Yes, you can do this. Yes, you did it." You also need to honor and support yourself for taking the time and energy to change and grow. Love yourself for the wonderful human being that you are. Pat yourself on the back; you did it.

And, like the butterfly—take flight. Spread your wings! Feel the joy of growth and rebirth.

EXERCISES

Write about a time when you went through a major transformation, such as a birth, death, moving, losing a job, problems in a relationship, or serious illness.

If you are going through a major transformation now, how can you spin your cocoon? Who can you reach out to for support? What boundaries do you need to set? How will you do this? Spend time in your comfort spot.

Look at your life. Is there room for growth? What can you do to transform?

Be kind to yourself as you go through this transformation. How can you nourish your body, heart, and soul? How can you find a bit of pleasure every day?

Cry. Rent a sad movie if you need some help.

Look back and see how you changed. Are you stronger? What have you learned about yourself? Write about the changes you notice.

Just when the caterpillar thought the world was over, it became a butterfly.

Anonymous

FOURTEEN

Smiles and Laughter

When was the last time you smiled? When was the last time you laughed? Have you noticed how a woman's face lights up when she smiles? Not only does a smile look great on the outside, but it also feels good on the inside.

How can you smile more often and let joy flow through your body? Let's practice. Go look in a mirror. Do a fake smile, just with your mouth, not with your eyes. How does it feel? You probably don't feel much. How does it look? Not very warm or friendly.

Now, smile at yourself from the inside. Close your eyes, think of something wonderful that fills you with joy, and when you feel a smile coming on, open your eyes and look at yourself. Don't you look great? How do you feel? Do you feel joy? This is what people see when you smile at them. Joy radiates off of you onto them—and that is what makes them smile in return.

How about putting a smile in your voice? My receptionist is beautiful, and becomes even more so when she smiles. My back is usually to her when I hear her on the phone, so I don't know for certain if she has a smile on her face, but it sounds like she does. A patient came in the other day with a gift for my receptionist, to thank her for her help. The woman had been anxious about an upcoming test and when she phoned the office, my receptionist was able to soothe and calm her. The patient said, "I felt so much better. I wanted to thank you."

How can you use your voice when you answer the phone or talk with your loved ones? How can you send a warm smile over the lines, which will make you and them feel great?

Learn to laugh often. Laughing relaxes muscles, eases tension, and releases all sorts of good chemicals. As the saying goes: laughter is the best medicine. If you can find humor in a serious situation, it helps the healing process. If you can laugh at yourself, even in a difficult circumstance, your life will be easier. You may not be able to find humor in a situation as you are going through it, but when you can, it will help you heal.

How else can you bring humor into your life? Watch funny movies and read books that make you laugh. Hanging out with children is another good way to bring laughter into your life. Children haven't figured out yet that life is serious—so they smile and laugh on a regular basis. They want to have fun and enjoy life. Children see the wonder of life and it makes them smile. Spend time in their world for a while and see what they experience. Embrace the joy that they feel.

EXERCISES

Stand in front of a mirror and see the difference between a fake smile and a real smile. Write about how they both feel.

Pick a day and give three people a fake smile and three people a real smile. Write about the reactions you get from the fake smiles and how it felt to you. Write about the reactions you received from the real smiles and how it felt.

The next time you answer the phone, put a smile on your face and in your voice. How does it feel?

Phone a friend. Put a smile in your voice and see how the conversation goes. Write about it.

Think of a difficult situation that happened in the past. Write about it and how devastated you were at the time. Then try to find some humor in it, now that you have made it through. Write about how you feel.

Spend time with someone who makes you laugh. Write about how you feel the next day. How can you do this more often?

How can you laugh more at work? Can you find humor as you go through your workday? Can you share humor with someone? Write about how your day goes when you can laugh instead of being serious all day.

Watch a funny movie or read a humorous book. Note how much better you feel.

Find a child and jump into his/her world for a while. How does it feel to look at the world with joy and wonder? How does it feel to smile and laugh frequently throughout the day? How can you do this on a regular basis? Write about what you saw and felt through the eyes of a child.

Because of your smile,
you make life more beautiful.

Thich Nhat Hanh

FIFTEEN

Forgiveness

"I will never forgive him for what he did to me." "I will never forgive her for what happened." How many times have you said this about someone? How does it feel when you remember past wrongs? Even though it could be something that happened last week, last month, or many years ago, the pain is agonizing and robs you of joy. Think about how much energy you expend thinking about something from the past that you cannot change. Imagine how free you would be if you let go of the negative feelings. Holding onto pain snatches the joy out of life. Forgive and release this person, this joy snatcher, and invite joy into your life.

This does not mean that what the person did was okay. But it's time to let go—for you. Forgiving is *for giving* to yourself. You waste an incredible amount of energy holding onto old hurts. Yes, it is important to digest what happened, and you might decide to seek counseling to get through it—but the time comes to let it go.

How much time have you spent thinking about that pain? Could you have used the time to focus on something positive? More pleasing? More fulfilling? Chances are, the person who did you wrong doesn't realize you're still holding onto the pain. Maybe you haven't seen him/her in a long time. Don't hold your breath waiting for him/her to apologize. Take charge of your life and let it go.

How about forgiving yourself? Is there something you did that you are flogging yourself about daily? Is it necessary to beat yourself up continually about something that already happened? Think about this for a while and consider having mercy on yourself as you so easily give mercy to others.

Forgiveness means taking back your life and releasing yourself from the pain. More than likely the person who hurt you is not bothered by the fact that you have not forgiven him/her, so the only one you are hurting is you. Forgiveness is about you. Release the negativity and let joy fill your life.

EXERCISES

Think of someone who hurt you and you have not forgiven. Write down what was done to you. Write down any triggers you can think of that bring this person back into your thoughts. Write down how you feel when you think of this person. If you are angry, look beyond the anger to see if it is a feeling of not being loved or respected by this person that bothers you. If this is the case, do your feelings change? If so, write about the difference and take a moment to soothe yourself if you realize it is a lack of love or respect and not anger.

When you remember the hurt of a past wrong, think about a person, place, or thing that makes you feel good. Then say: "I release _____. I am free and I am loved (sometimes just saying this when the person comes to mind is helpful). I replace _____ with _____ (whatever feels good). Write down how this feels.

Finally, fill in the blanks below, sign the release, and then read it out loud.

I commit to myself to release _____
from my life and fill the space that _____
has held in my life with _____.

Signed: _____
Date:_____

How does it feel when you read this out loud? Write about your feelings. Do this every day for two weeks. Maybe you will change what you write in the empty space or you might keep it the same for the two weeks. Write about how you felt at the beginning of this exercise and at the end of two weeks.

Do you need to forgive yourself for something that you did? How can you have mercy and forgive yourself as you would another who had done the same thing? Write about what you did and the words you would use to forgive someone who had done the same thing. Apply those words to yourself. Write about how you feel.

♡

How does one know if she has forgiven?
You tend to feel sorrow over the
circumstance instead of rage, you tend
to feel sorry for the person rather than
angry with him. You tend to have
nothing left to say about it all.

Clarissa Pinkola Estés, PhD

SIXTEEN

Namasté:
Send Loving Thoughts

♡

Namasté is the most popular greeting in India. It is actually a submission, a surrendering, an honoring of the person you are addressing. Americans don't usually consider submitting or surrendering to another person as a positive act; but Namasté is.

There are many definitions of Namasté. My two favorites are: "I salute the divinity within you" and "The divine in me honors the divine in you." How often, when you think of another person, do you experience love, light, peace, and truth in your heart? When you feel this way for another person, you also have those feelings for yourself—and that is good.

How can you send loving thoughts to those that you love on a regular basis? How can you radiate love for the people you hold dear when you see them? How can you honor your enemies and people you don't like? (When you send bad energy to those you don't like, you experience the bad energy too. Not a pleasant thought, is it?)

Think of someone you care for a great deal. Think Namasté, the divine in me honors the divine in you. How does this feel? Pretty good, right? The next time you see this person, radiate love from your heart. Note their reaction and how you feel.

Then think of someone with whom you are angry. How do you feel? Not so good, right? Visualize this person in your mind and send them the Namasté greeting. (There is the divine in everyone—even though it may seem like a small amount.) How does it feel to send this person loving thoughts? Does it feel better than when you send negative thoughts? Start saying Namasté to this person whenever he/she pops into your mind. Feel yourself sending the divine energy from you to the divine part of them. It will make you feel better.

Sending negative energy makes you feel terrible, likewise sending positive energy will make you feel better. It might take lots of practice before you can send Namasté greetings—but keep practicing. The results will be worthwhile.

Where else can you use Namasté in your life? Try it when you're waiting in traffic or in line at the grocery store. Send Namasté to those around you. It feels so much better than to get irritated that you're not moving faster.

As you practice this, your light will shine—and your life will fill with joy.

EXERCISES

Select the definition of Namasté you like best or a different greeting, such as "I send you peace, love and joy;" or "Blessings to you;" or "God bless you." Write it down. Then say it out loud three times. Write down how you feel

Think of someone you care for very much. Imagine greeting him or her with Namasté or other warm words. Write down how it feels.

Think of someone you don't like much. Visualize saying Namasté or another warm greeting to him or her. Are you able to do it? Do you feel resistance? (When you feel resistance, you are blocking out joy.) Keep practicing. Write down how it feels.

Practice sending Namasté or another greeting when you are standing in line or waiting in traffic. Write down how you feel when you do this.

The next time you see someone you are upset with, send him or her Namasté from your heart to his or hers. Take a breath, feel warmth in your heart, and send it to his or her heart. Doesn't this feel better than resisting any feelings or sending bad thoughts toward that person? Keep practicing and it will get easier. Write down how it felt the first time you did this. Then write down how it felt the tenth time.

I honor in you the divine that I honor within myself. I know we are one.

Deepak Chopra

SEVENTEEN

The Mind

The mind is a powerful tool. It can bring you joy or absolute devastation. Take a few moments to sit still. What thoughts fill your mind? Are they positive or negative? Many times when you are quiet for a moment, your mind fills with negative thoughts, such as what you should be doing, something bad that happened yesterday, or something that could happen in the future. The goal is to begin to invite joy into your life and fill your mind with pleasurable thoughts on a regular basis.

There are several techniques you can use to change negative thoughts to positive ones. They take much effort; but the more you practice them, the easier it gets. These techniques include letting go, the critic and the nurturer, and being your best friend.

Let's start with letting go. People often say: "Just let it go" or

"Just get over it." It sounds easy; although in reality it is not. When someone has done something to you that you don't like or you have done something you regret, how often do you think about it? When you are in a difficult situation, do you find your mind consumed with the event? You might even realize you should let it go—but it just won't go away. You can't stop thinking about it. What can you do?

First, stop running these negative and upsetting thoughts through your mind like a gerbil on a treadmill and begin to speak them out loud. When you're finished whining and complaining to friends, family, and anyone who will listen, write down the issue several times to release it from your mind. As you write, think of solutions. You may want to talk to a trusted friend or a counselor. Find someone who is objective and can help you walk through the situation. You need to come to a resolution in your mind. If you don't, it could haunt you for the rest of your life.

As you talk with people, listen to yourself. After you have written about the issue, read what you wrote. Keep doing this as you talk and write about the issue. After awhile you may get sick of hearing yourself talk about it and become tired of reading about the same old issue—then you can let it go.

If you are still holding on to an old hurt, go back to Chapter 15. It is time to let it go. You are wasting the precious time you have on earth. Even if you cannot change the situation, you can certainly release yourself from it.

Remember, the only way to let something go is to replace it with something else. If you release a negative thought from your mind it leaves an empty space. If you do not fill that space, the negative thought will come back. Review Chapters 5 and 6. Use your mind to make you feel good instead of obsessing about something that makes you feel bad.

The second technique is the critic and the nurturer. Start by listening to the negative thoughts in your head. Then work with them in the following manner: first regard these thoughts as the voice of someone in your past or present life who was/is negative towards you. Once you've done this there are two techniques you can use to stop the voice. The first one is to acknowledge that person by saying: "Thank you very much for that information. I will take it under consideration." This stops the voice for a minute and gives you time to think about something positive.

The second technique is one Sandra Hines taught me. You begin by visualizing this person and all the negative things they are saying to you. Then imagine a hallway with many doors. You say to this person, "Down the hall, at the end, on the right, is a room where there are a lot of people who would love to hear what you have to say." This person looks at you excitedly and says, "Really?" You nod yes. Then you visualize him walking down the hallway. As he gets to the last door and reaches for the knob he looks back at you for confirmation that this is the correct door. You nod yes again. As he opens the door there is round of applause for him and he smiles a great big smile and walks in, closing the door behind him. You are free from his negativity for a moment.

At this point you want to be ready to fill the void with your nurturer. She can be someone from your past or present life who has had a positive influence on you (or it can be someone you make up). You will visualize her saying something positive, like "You are doing a great job" or "You are a wonderful person" or "You are so loved" or "You are a great mom, daughter, wife, employee, housekeeper . . ." Then revel in those good thoughts.

Is this craziness? Maybe, but it sure is fun sending that negative person down the hallway and then filling up with good thoughts from your nurturer.

The key to recognizing the critic is that he makes you feel bad. The nurturer loves you unconditionally and makes you feel great. You are too hard on yourself, which is why oftentimes you fail or don't even try. You would never consider saying to others what you say to yourself. You can be everyone else's nurturer, yet beat yourself up on a daily basis. It is time to stop this behavior and be as good to you as you are to others.

The final technique is being your own best friend. When you are struggling with a problem, step out of yourself and think about what you would say to your dearest friend if she were experiencing the same thing. The beauty of this technique is that you know exactly what you would tell your dearest friend, the difficulty is following your own good advice. Treating yourself with kindness and understanding is an amazing experience!

The mind is a powerful tool and it can stop you from living a life of joy by keeping you mired in the muddy waters of negativity. Take control of your mind today.

EXERCISES

Pay attention to your thoughts. Listen to them. After a few days write down the thought that you dwell on the most.

Journal about the situation that is most mind-consuming. Talk to a friend or a counselor to find out what options you have to deal with the situation. Write them down—and do them.

Once you have followed through on your options, stop thinking about the situation. When the situation pops into your head, as it will, think about the option that you have chosen to follow.

If there are no options, think of someone or something that is important to you and let the negative thought go. Write down five good thoughts you can fill your mind with. Practice them and write how it feels.

Describe or draw your critic.

Describe or draw your nurturer.

Describe a situation where you can use your critic and nurturer. Write about how it feels to send the critic down the hallway. How did it feel to fill up with the nurturer's words?

Describe a situation that troubles you. Then step out of yourself and pretend that your dearest friend is in this situation. How would you counsel her? Write down some steps that you can take to begin moving away from this situation.

You cannot control what happens to you, but you can control your attitude toward what happens to you and in that you will be mastering change rather than allowing it to master you.

Brian Tracey

EIGHTEEN

Think and Feel Joy

If you fill your mind with positive thoughts, good things will come to you. This is taken from the law of physics that says like attracts like.

How often have you awakened in the morning feeling rotten and, as the day progressed, more events occurred that made you feel worse? How many times have you awakened in a good mood and great things happened all day long?

The wonderful thing about this law is it gives you power to change. If you feel like you are headed for a bad day, change your attitude and fill your mind with joyful thoughts. With positive thought, it is possible to change a bad day into a good day.

To apply this technique, you must first pay attention to your thoughts. You will probably find that your thoughts are either in the past or future and they are not happy ones. The next step is to think about something that feels good until you feel joy in your heart. (The feeling part is important.) You can think about a puppy, a kitten, your child, white fluffy clouds in a clear blue sky, etc. Whenever you catch yourself pondering something negative, think of that which makes you feel good. Make sure you feel the warmth of joy in your heart, as this is critical.

Although this seems like a simple technique, it can be difficult to practice. You will find times when your mind says: "I have a right to be upset about this" or "I have a right to think these negative thoughts" or "I have a right to feel bad."

Yes, you have the right to feel bad and there are days when you just need to wallow in self-pity—but not most days. Some days it will take a lot of effort to keep positive feelings alive in your heart. Sandra Hines said to me the other day, "Suffer as little as you like." You deserve to feel good. You deserve joy, and it feels so much better." Practice this technique as often as you can—and it will have a positive impact on your life.

EXERCISES

Make a list of ten people or things that make you feel good. Put the list in your wallet.

Pay attention to your thoughts for a couple of days. How do your thoughts make you feel? Write about the negative thoughts and how they make you feel. Write about the positive thoughts and how they make you feel. Where do you sense these feelings? In your heart, your gut, or somewhere else?

Replace negative thoughts with thoughts that make you feel good. Write down how it feels to do this.

Every time you are in your car and every time you go to the bathroom, think about something good. This will change the stress level you may feel when you are driving. And the bathroom is a great place to escape to when you are in a difficult or negative situation. Think of something good and change your energy. Write down some examples of how you changed your negative thoughts to positive ones.

Pay attention to how your days start and end. See how the rule "like attracts like" works in your life. Write about what you discover. (Usually you can see how this rule works much better in other people's lives. Observe others, and then take an honest look at yourself.)

Practice positive thinking to change your days from not going well to going really well. How does it feel? Write about it.

In times of joy, all of us wished
we possessed a tail we could wag.

W.H. Auden

The Beat of Joy

There is a beat I love to hear
It means that joy is somewhere near.
Sometimes she's fast and makes me dance.
Sometimes she's slow and brings a trance.

It's up to me to hear her call,
To let her rise, to let her fall,
To ride her wave, to feel her pull,
To let her come and make me full.

So calm, so sweet,
Oh what a treat,
She often sweeps me
Off my feet.

And when I feel
Her gentle shove
I float, I bask
In warmth and love.

~ SANDRA HINES

NINETEEN

Why? Why? Why?

How many times have you asked yourself why something bad happens? "Why did this have to happen to me?" "Why is this happening to me again?"

Have you ever received an answer to these questions? Probably not. At least not when you were going through the difficult situation. Sometimes, after you have fully recovered and if you are paying attention, you may discover why certain life events happened to you. But, for the most part, asking why things happen will do nothing but snatch joy from your life.

Instead of "whying" yourself into misery, ask yourself: "What can I do about this problem?" or "What is the lesson I am supposed to learn?" or "Have I been in a similar situation before?" Asking how you can resolve a problem will bring you some answers and allows you to take action to move away from the situation. As you release this situation and move away from the whys, joy can return to your life.

Two other questions to ask are: "How has this situation changed my life" and "Where do I want to go from here?" You might think your life is ruined and there is nowhere to go from here. But, after a while you need to realize that ranting and raving takes you nowhere. It keeps you feeling miserable. There comes a time when you must stop feeling sorry for yourself and take action.

You may want to have an actual pity party. You can invite your friends over, eat chocolate or drink wine, and whine about what has happened to you. After your pity party, however, it is time to decide what you can do about this problem. It is time to decide where you want to go from here. You may even end the pity party by having your friends brainstorm about some solutions.

When you do this, you gain incredible insight into your behavior and you can feel empowered to change. Even though these insights can be painful, you must spend time in solitude and find the answers.

As you experience challenges, know it takes time to heal. It takes solitude, rest, taking care of your body, and sometimes seeking professional help to work through the difficult events of life. If you choose to skip the process, stuff your feelings, and avoid grieving, the pain will come out in different ways. You may feel anger, depression, anxiety, or develop an illness. Acknowledge the pain, rest, take care of your body, and seek comfort and support.

Remember, life is an ongoing process. Everything happens for a reason. (Of course, it is much easier to see this when it happens to someone else.) Even after you think you have learned a lesson, you might be tested one, two, or three more times. This is to make sure you are clear about what you were supposed to learn and that you grow and evolve spiritually.

You are given opportunities to get to know your true self. Once you learn these lessons, they resolve and you do not have to repeat them, but it takes time.

Think of life as an upward spiral. You keep spiraling up but you also keep coming around to similar situations. However, each time you spiral upward, you are a little wiser. In time, you can get the lesson and be free from this particular life situation. Pay attention when you hear yourself say, "I can't believe this is happening to me again." When you hear yourself say this, it is time to look closely at what is happening so you learn from the situation that keeps repeating itself.

There are two ways to learn your lessons. One is by saying: "I am not going there anymore" and the other is with the mirror technique. The I-am-not-going-there-anymore technique must be implemented as soon as a situation repeats itself. You must take action before you get too deep into the event. It involves listening to your intuition when it tells you something is not quite right. It means not repeating a behavior when something doesn't feel right—even if you can't give a specific reason why it feels wrong. Many times when you move away from a situation that your gut tells you to avoid, you will never know why.

I recently attended a workshop on "Creating Fulfilling Relationships" by Michael Mirdad PhD. His view on life is that God is first, self is second, and others are third. When you are in a difficult situation with another person you need to take time for yourself to ask if the situation is working for you. If it is not working for you, you need to determine what will work for you. Or, as a dear friend of mine states: "This is what I require." Then you go to God and find peace with this answer. Then you go to the other person and have a discussion. If you cannot find a way to work through the situation so that it works for you, it is time to go, or be miserable for the rest of your life, or keep wondering why this is happening to you.

It sounds simple, doesn't it? It is very simple—but also probably the hardest thing you will do because it requires you to do what is right for you and not what is right for someone else. It is time to ask "Why am I in this situation again?" and figure out what it is that you require. Then, follow through by speaking up for your self and getting the respect and love you deserve.

I was telling this to a minister's wife the other day. She said, "I have the God and others figured out, but I have been forgetting about my self." I think this is true for a lot of women.

There is another question to ask yourself: "Is this working for me?" If the answer is no, move on to: "This is what I require." Determine what it is that you require. Now, here's the big question: "Is my request unreasonable?"

I would venture to guess that nine times out of ten your request is not unreasonable. Go forth to others and make your desires known and expect that you will get your needs met Then watch how your life changes as you invite the joy of honoring yourself into your life.

The other method is the mirror technique. This can be painful, but it works. During my certification program for Deepak Chopra's "Creating Health" course, our instructor defined the mirror technique this way: if there is a personality characteristic in another person that drives you crazy, that personality trait is a part of you and until you can forgive it in you, you will never forgive it in another.

The next time someone does something that makes you angry, look for that behavior in *your* personality. Your ego will immediately jump in and say, "I am never like that." Keep on searching and eventually you will find it. What can you do about this behavior in yourself? As you work on you more, you will find you have a lot less time to judge other people's activities.

Have you ever noticed that when you point a finger at someone, if you flip your hand over, there are three fingers pointing back at you? Try it.

Sometimes predicaments occur that are totally out of your control. Everyone experiences challenges. When you do, you need to walk through them consciously and ask for support and guidance. When you do this, you can rediscover the simple pleasures of living.

One avenue of support is talking with a spiritual director. A spiritual director is defined by Jeffrey S. Gaines, MDiv, as one who "companions another person, listening to the person's life story with an ear for the movement of the Holy, of the Divine." I have been working with a spiritual director for the last two years. My spiritual director provides a sacred space and assistance in finding the wisdom within as I walk my path on earth. It is a powerful experience.

Look at the challenging events in your life as lessons and opportunities to learn about your true self. As you come through each lesson, another one arises. Will you allow circumstances to make you bitter for the rest of your life or will you pick yourself up and begin doing the work to invite joy back into your life?

EXERCISES

Think of a situation that still causes you to ask "Why did this happen to me?" Does this situation keep occurring in your life? Write all your thoughts and feelings about it.

Consider what you can do about the situation, how it has changed your life, and where you want to go from here. Write about your thoughts.

Write down three small steps you can take to change the situation or determine where you can go from here. Take one step per day or one step per week. Write down how you feel after each step, how you feel after the third step, and how the situation or your perception of the situation has changed.

Pick another situation. Ask yourself the following questions: Is this working for me? What do I require? Is this reasonable? Take some time to find peace with your answers. Then have a discussion with the other person. Write about how it went as you came from the powerful place of honoring yourself.

The next time you point your finger at another about his or her terrible behavior, turn your hand over and look at the three fingers pointing at you. How can you begin to change your life so you are coming from a joyful place instead of a judgmental one?

If you are going through a devastating time, I ask that you reach out and seek support and solace from someone. It may be a counselor, a spiritual director, or your church. You are not meant to go through life alone. There are people who can help.

*I just realized there's going to be
a lot of painful times in life, so I had
better learn to deal with it right away.*

Trey Parker and Matt Stone

TWENTY

What's Right Instead of What's Wrong

How often do you find yourself complaining about a situation? How often do you hear yourself say: "He did this" or "She did that"? Do you complain about the same thing—that never changes? How do you feel when you whine and complain? Probably not so good. There is not much joy involved when you complain instead of focus on what is right.

Let's begin with relationships. What is wrong with your husband, your child, your family? Most people can come up with a long list of complaints. Can you make an equally long list about what is right with your husband, your children, and your family? With practice you can learn to focus on what is right with your loved ones—and when you do this, joy will enter your life.

To begin, look at what is wrong with your loved ones. If you are not getting love and respect from them, then something needs to change. Yelling at the top of your lungs or slamming doors will not get them to change. To get people to behave differently, or at least hear you, takes an objective plan and a calm voice. It also takes being ready to follow through with consequences if the other person cannot meet what it is that you are asking for. This is not a control issue. If your needs are not being met and the person keeps promising they will change—but they don't—what are you going to do? You can stay in the relationship and be miserable or you can go. Your choice. (I strongly suggest counseling, so you have an objective professional help you make a plan to get your needs met.)

Next, think about what is right with your loved ones. It helps if you make a list because when you write things down, they become more firmly embedded in your mind. As you write this list, think hard about the person. What brought him or her into your life? What did you like about him or her then, what do you like about him or her now? How can you get to know this person better so you can discover more good? People are in your life for a reason, either to support you or to teach you some lessons.

Start telling your loved ones what is right about them. If you have been on a major rampage regarding what is wrong with everyone, you may get a variety of reactions. The reactions can include shock, disbelief, suspicion, and even joy. People may wonder what you are up to when you say something nice to them. That's all right, they'll get used to it.

I also want you to notice how you feel when you say nice things to people. At first, there may be some resistance because that long list of what's wrong is still in your head. You may say out loud to your husband: "I really appreciate the fact that you take care of the lawn." But in your head, you are

thinking ". . . but you don't help out with this and that."
Complimenting people takes practice. Appreciate people for
who they are and what they do. Fill your head and heart with
kind thoughts of appreciation, and eventually the list in your
head of what's wrong will get quieter.

Put yourself in their shoes for a minute. Think about the last
time someone told you that you were doing a good job. How
did that make you feel? Think about the last time someone said
you were doing something wrong. It didn't feel so good, did it?
You *can* change someone's life by supporting her in what she
does. You can also change it when you don't support her.

You should also realize that what you give out comes back
to you. It may take time and it may come from another source,
but if you are supportive, the support will be returned to you.

This technique can be used on everyone, even strangers.
Do you complain a lot at work? If so, you need to look for
what is right about your job instead of what is wrong with it. If
there is nothing right with your job, then you need to look for
another one. Pay attention at work. You might be surprised at
how many things you can find that are good about your job.
When you focus on what is right, what is wrong can fade
away.

How can you spread good cheer among your co-workers?
You can say things like: "That shirt looks really nice on you" or
"I really appreciated your help yesterday."

Are you ready to focus on what is right in your life instead
of what is wrong? Are you ready to feel joy instead of doom
and gloom?

EXERCISES

Make a list of what is wrong about your immediate family members. If there are some big issues that need to be looked at, now is the time to make some changes. Verbalize your needs. If this is not effective, seek counseling.

Make a list of what is right about your family members.

Tell each of your family members one thing that is right with them every day for one week. Write down their reactions. Write down how you felt when you complimented them. Note any changes that occurred during the week.

Write down what is right about your job and co-workers.

Before you go to work each day for a week, think about one thing you like about your job. Write it down and focus on that thought throughout the day. Say one nice thing to a co-worker each day this same week. Note his or her reaction, and yours. Write about how it felt to focus on the good instead of the bad.

Write down twenty things that are right with your life. This may take some time. It is easy to miss all the wonder that is available to you.

Each day for a week, focus on one different thing that is right with your life. Write down what you are focusing on that day and then write about how you feel.

Fill your mind with light, happiness, hope, feelings of security, and strength— and soon your life will reflect these qualities.

Remez Sassonh

Twenty-One

Present Moment

Where are you right now? Are you present in the now? What is it like to be in the present moment? How do you feel?

It is amazing how your thoughts can take you anywhere but here. Most people rarely spend time in the present—usually they are concerned about the past or the future. What a waste of time. You cannot change the past. The present is where you live. You can have an impact on your future by having positive or negative thoughts. Feeling good in the present can bring more joy in the future. Being miserable in the present can project more misery into the future.

Start to pay attention to what you are doing moment-to-moment—and let the joyful aspects of the moment fill you. Watch this joy manifest more joy in your future.

The first step towards living in the present is awareness. You may want to practice by checking your thoughts every hour to see where you really are. Once you are aware that you are not in the present moment, remind yourself where you are. Then, look at your surroundings and say to yourself, "Here I am." Feel your feet on the ground; this can bring you to the present. Feel your heart and feel joy because you are here. Take a deep breath, release it, and enjoy the present. How does it feel? Not too bad, does it?

This does not mean you should not plan for your future; but trouble begins when you become rigidly attached to having your life go exactly as you plan. Life rarely occurs as you expect and you can experience all sorts of grief if you expect things to happen exactly as you wish. You can, however, make general plans, take action towards goals, and then step back and see what happens. Usually it's better than what you imagined.

Have you ever wondered why you have vivid childhood memories but not so many memories as an adult? It is because children live in the present moment. When children do something, they are there, right now. They are living, breathing, and feeling the moment. As adults, we usually do not. To make a memory, stop, look at the situation, and utilize all of your senses—feel it. Then you will remember it.

Even though this is an easy concept, adults rarely do it— except for painful events. We feel those completely and we remember them for life.

How can you remember the good times, the joys in your life? It takes intention and practice. Find someone or something in nature that brings you pleasure. Really look at this person or object and let the warm feeling in your heart build as you love the person or object. Hold on to the feeling and then take a deep breath. Now, close your eyes. Can you still see it and feel it? That is a memory.

Stop, look, and feel every day, every moment of your life. Fill yourself with joy.

EXERCISES

What are you doing right now? (Obviously, reading this book.) Look around you, plant your feet on the ground, see where you are, feel where you are, and use all of your senses. How do you feel?

Take one week to work at being in the present moment. Write down your experiences. Note that the more you practice this concept, the easier it becomes. Be aware that when you start, you might only accomplish a few minutes in the present—but keep at it. Eventually you will spend less time in the past and future.

Make a memory. Find a person or an object in nature and focus on it. Feel the warmth in your heart as you focus on this person or object. Use all of your senses. What do you see, feel, hear, smell, and taste? Hold the sensation for as long as you can, then take a deep breath. Close your eyes. Can you still feel and see the person or object? Tomorrow, remember that person or object and the feeling you experienced. Write about your new memory and how it feels.

Work on living in the present for the rest of your life. Whenever you catch yourself going to the past or future, return to the present.

When you attend an event, make the intention that you will be present throughout the entire event. Write about what this experience is like for you.

*Learning to live in the present moment
is part of the path to joy.*

Sarah Ban Breathnach

TWENTY-TWO

Live as if Every Day Were Your Last

♡

What if today was your last day on earth? What would you do if you weren't going to be here tomorrow? Think of the people you care for. Think about the activities you wanted to do but have not yet done. If you only had a short time to live, what would you do?

Do you just get through each day on automatic pilot, then wake up the next morning and start all over again? When was the last time you appreciated the people around you—and told them so? When was the last time you really noticed your family or friends?

Take a moment to think about this. When was the last time you told the people around you that you loved them, that you appreciated them, and that you were glad they were in your life? How would they feel if you died tomorrow and you had not told them?

Appreciate the people in your life today, instead of waiting for a crisis to occur. What can you say to your children, your spouse, your family, your friends, and your co-workers to let them know you care? What can you do that will make them feel special? (It will also make you feel good when you do and say things from the heart.)

If you haven't made a habit of appreciating people, you may get some shocked looks—but that's okay—keep talking. Give your kids a hug or a pat on the back and say "I love you". Tell your spouse you appreciate what he does for you and tell him you love him. Remember, this could be your last day on earth.

Do you have siblings, parents, or extended family you can call to tell them you are glad they are in your life? That you love them? (A word of caution: My daughter and I like to watch the TV show *Seventh Heaven*. In one episode, a man was told he needed open-heart surgery. He was so afraid he was going to die that he didn't tell his family he was having surgery. He did, however, phone the people close to him to say he loved them; but he did not tell them about his upcoming operation. His brother-in-law knew something was wrong because people generally don't phone to say I love you. After confronting him, he found out about the surgery and convinced the man to tell his family. He did, got their support, and came through the surgery with flying colors. So, when you phone people, assure them that you are fine and only doing an exercise in a book.)

Hopefully you will not take this opportunity to tell off anyone. If you have the urge to do so, re-read Chapter 11—and let those people go, immediately.

Focus on the feelings you keep inside and don't express. Say "Why not!" and let your feelings come out. Think about how the world would be if everyone spoke from his or her heart on a daily basis. Imagine the joy.

Do you frequently speak in anger and fear, and not consider where the other person is coming from? To speak from love, you must pause for a moment, feel the warmth in your heart, and let the words come from there instead of from your head or ego.

Think of words you would like to hear from a loved one. How can you speak those words? Consider what the other person needs and give them words of encouragement. It may be easier to do this if you considered today as if it were your last day on earth. There would be so much you would want to say.

If you died tomorrow, what regrets would you have? What do you want to do in this lifetime? Read your notes from Chapters 5 and 6. Are you doing any of these things? What steps can you take to do what you really want to do? Now is the time to move toward your dreams. Remember, it is never too late to make your dreams come true.

Live in joy by speaking your feelings and following your bliss each and every day of your life.

EXERCISES

Today is your last day on earth. Think about your immediate family. What can you say to them that expresses how you feel about them? Write down what you would say and whom you would say it to. Do it; then write down their reactions. Write down how it made you feel.

Today is your last day on earth. Think about your extended family. Who would you phone to say thanks for being in your life? Write down what you said and to whom. Write down their reactions and how this made you feel.

Today is your last day on earth. What positive things would you say to your co-workers and to those you meet throughout the day? Let go of any negative stuff.

If you have negative thoughts about someone, write down what you'd like to say to them. When you are finished, rip it up or burn the paper to release the negativity.

Today is the last day of your life. Write down any regrets. What do you wish to do that you haven't yet done? Write down the steps you can take to make your dreams come true.

Choose a day next week and pretend it is your last day on earth. Do it from a place of pure joy. For the duration of this day, believe that you are going on the most incredible journey. This day you will speak fully and completely from your heart. How do you treat those around you? Write about the reactions you inspire and how you feel. Then make a pact to live as if every day were your last.

Too often we underestimate the power of a touch, a smile, a kind word, a listening ear, an honest compliment, or the smallest act of caring, all of which have the potential to turn a life around.

Leo Buscagli

TWENTY-THREE

Puttering

♡

When was the last time you puttered around your home? Have you ever puttered around your home? Do you know what *puttering* means? The *American Heritage Dictionary* defines *puttering* as "to occupy oneself in an aimless manner."

To putter is to wander around your home looking at things, maybe rearranging something, with no goal in mind. It may be cleaning out a drawer or a closet. The important aspect of puttering is there should be no stress or hurry to the task. When was the last time you puttered?

In Greek mythology, Hestia is the goddess of hearth and home. She is responsible for the hearth fire and the contentment and sacredness you feel when you putter around your home. When you arrive home after a day at the office or a vacation, Hestia inspires the thought: "I am home, blessed be." It is the pure joy of mundane, everyday living.

When you perform everyday tasks—cooking, cleaning, laundry, etc.—let Hestia in. Feel her energy, focus on the routine, and feel joy. Relax. Breathe. Play some quiet music. Be in the present moment. Time itself will slow down. It is an incredible concept and one well worth trying.

Pay attention to how you and your family feel when you putter. The more you slow down, the more joy everyone experiences.

Hestia is responsible for the contentment and peace that fills a home. How does your home feel? Is it chaotic and in an uproar most of the time? When you visit your comfort spot, concentrate on Hestia and look for guidance on making your home calmer.

Puttering brings joy and honor to the daily tasks of women. Mundane everyday tasks, when done with intention, will bring peace into your environment and you. Pay homage to the daily work—allow yourself time to putter.

EXERCISES

Pick one household task you can do in a slow, intentional way. Ask Hestia for guidance. Focus on what you are doing, take your time, and see how it feels to putter. Write about what you did and how it felt.

Commit to puttering at least thirty minutes each day for one week. Vary the tasks you select. Write about what you did and how it felt. At the end of the week can you notice any change in how your home environment feels?

Let Hestia's calm accompany you when you perform the mundane tasks of everyday life. Notice how your house begins to feel more like a home, a place full of peace and comfort.

Puttering is really a time to be alone, to dream, and to get in touch with yourself.

Alexandra Stoddard

TWENTY-FOUR

Do What You Loved To Do as a Child

Let me begin this chapter by acknowledging the sad reality that some of you had traumatic childhoods and therefore do not have happy memories to choose from for this exercise. If this is your situation, is there anything that helped you survive, like reading, riding your bike, going to the lake, talking with classmates, etc.?

If there is nothing in your childhood that you loved, was there something you wanted to do? Can you bring that into your life now? If there was nothing pleasant in your youth, then spend time watching children play today. Maybe their play will inspire something in you. Or grab a box of crayons and start to color. Coloring is soothing and can open your mind to activities you might like to try.

Now, for the exercise: take a moment to think about your childhood. What did you love to do? Was it swimming, reading, walking downtown, chatting with girlfriends, sailing, etc.? If you enjoyed going to the beach, and haven't been there in many years, go today and see how it feels. Enjoy the warm sand between your toes, the aroma of the water, and the laughter of nearby children. Experience a simple joy from your childhood.

If you loved riding your bicycle—go for a bike ride tonight. If you don't have a bicycle, purchase one. Feel the freedom of being outdoors with the wind in your face.

Do you think you're too old to resort to your childhood activities? Well, you're not. Get rid of that thought. You are never too old to have fun. In fact, not having fun makes you old. You were not meant to only work. All work and no play makes Jill a dull girl. Remember that!

Lighten up. Bring back the pleasures you enjoyed as a child. Return to the world of childlike activity—it is a magical place. When you slow down long enough to go for a bike ride or to the beach, you will experience joy.

Life is short. Bring back what you once enjoyed.

EXERCISES

What did you love to do as a child? Write down everything that comes to mind. Then, look at the list. Which activities, if any, do you enjoy as an adult?

What steps can you take to bring that joy back into your life?

Make a promise to your Self that you will keep this activity in your life—you will do it more than once. Get out your calendar and write down in ink for the next three months when you will do this activity. Then, do it! Write down how it feels to do what you love the first four times that you do it.

If you had an awful childhood and can think of nothing that you loved as a child, go to the store and buy the largest box of crayons and a coloring book. Take a half-hour, in silence or with soft music playing, and color. See what thoughts come to mind. There may be tears; let them flow and see what follows. Write about your thoughts.

The child within you has what it takes
to envision and manifest ANYTHING!
. . . Let your inner kid out of you
and give yourself expression!
You are a child of the universe—
if you can imagine it, you can be it!

Greg Barette

TWENTY-FIVE

Nature

♡

When was the last time you enjoyed the simplicity and glory of Mother Nature? Do you ever go outside and stay for a while? When was the last time you actually looked at the sky, the trees, or the flowers? When was the last time you listened to the birds or water lapping onto a shoreline?

If you live in a city, visit the park. If you live in a rural area, just take a walk. Wherever it is, the next time you step outdoors, stop. Look. Listen. Breathe. Use your senses to see, feel, hear, and smell. Look around with childlike wonder and see how beautiful Mother Nature is.

Mother Nature has many offerings. Water is healing, regardless if it's an ocean, lake, river, or stream. You can do several things with water. You can watch the waves roll in and the sun sparkle off its surface. You can smell it. You can touch it. You can play in it. You can even float on it in a boat or canoe. Allowing water to caress your body is soothing. It can feel as though your troubles are being washed away.

What kind of water do you like to be near? Is it the awesome ocean or the Great Lakes or a small inland lake? Do you prefer to be in the woods near a river or a small stream? How can you visit water areas more often?

When was the last time you watched a tree swaying in the breeze or stretched out on the grass and listened to rustling leaves? As you're driving, do you ever notice sunlight playing in the treetops? When was the last time you were awed by the beauty of a fall color tour?

There are so many different flowers and plants—which are your favorites? Is it a rose? A daisy? A tulip? Lilacs? Are you attracted to their fragrance or design? Have you ever planted an herb garden? Lavender and rosemary are two of the most aromatic. Put your hands lightly together near the base of the herb and run them up the plant. The scent will get on your hands and is truly glorious.

If you live near mountains, take time to appreciate their majesty.

Mother Nature also provides rain and snow. Which one is your favorite? Have you ever seen the sun sparkle on freshly fallen snow or taken a nap to the sound of the rain gently falling on the rooftop? Magnificent! A great way to enjoy snow is to go snowshoeing or cross-country skiing.

What do you smell when you are outside? There is nothing like the fresh spring air or the earthiness after a hard rain. When was the last time you built a campfire on a cool summer evening? Do you like the mixture of the smoke and the crisp air?

What do you feel when you are outside? How does the soil

feel when you plant flowers? Do you like the coolness of the grass on your bare feet or do you prefer the warmth of sand? Have you ever let snowflakes fall gently on your face? Have you ever tasted a snowflake? Do you stop and let the breeze blow away your troubles and clear your mind?

We are not meant to be indoors all the time. Get out into nature. Focus on something different each time you go out and vary the places you go. Let Mother Nature fill you with joy.

EXERCISES

Go outside every day for one week. Write down what you see, smell, hear, and touch. What was it like being in nature? Did it affect your day in any way?

Decide how you can spend more time in nature. Write about how you will achieve this.

It was a lovely day of blue skies and gentle breezes. Bees buzzed, birds tootled, and squirrels bustled to and fro, getting their sun-tan in the bright sunshine. In a word all Nature smiled.

P.G. Wodehouse

151

TWENTY-SIX

Using Your Senses

♡

Humans have five senses: seeing, hearing, smelling, touching, and tasting. When your senses encounter pleasing sensations, you can feel pure and absolute joy. In contrast, when unpleasant sensations intrude, your lifeblood can be drained.

Your senses and past experiences cause you to perceive life differently than other people. What you see, hear, touch, smell, and taste is your unique expression in this world. It is important to honor how you feel when your senses are stimulated.

You have the ability to change how you perceive the world through your senses by paying attention to your reactions when your senses are stimulated, and making changes as needed.

You have the ability to control what stimulates your senses. You have the ability to heal yourself and others by using things that are soothing to the senses. You have the ability to choose what you like instead of following someone else's path. Change your environment and you can alter your life.

> *Nothing can cure the soul but the senses,*
> *just as nothing can cure the senses*
> *but the soul.*

Oscar Wilde

WHAT DO YOU SEE?

Look around you. Do you see anything pleasing? If not, close your eyes for a moment and then open them again. Look for one thing that gives you pleasure. If there is truly nothing, then try another room or location. Focus on whatever you see that gives you pleasure. Is it something that brings back memories of a good time? Is it something that is pretty and the colors make you feel good? Keep focusing on it and let warmth enter your chest. It may be just a flicker, but you'll feel it. Try to expand on it.

If you don't find anything that brings you pleasure in your home or office you should ask yourself why. Sometimes you need to discover what you don't like before you can figure out what you do like.

What changes can you make to your environment so it is more pleasing to you? It could be as easy as rearranging the furniture, getting rid of knickknacks, repainting the walls, or new flooring. Your environment is a reflection of you and how you feel inside. What is being reflected when you look around? How does your environment make you feel inside? Is it time to take some action?

You don't have to spend a lot of money. Try adding a candle in a blue glass holder to the room. Candlelight and the color blue are healing. Light the candle and focus on it for a while. Feel the light and warmth in your heart center, and let it flow throughout your body.

Likewise, if your work area needs soothing touches, make some alterations. Try bringing something from home that is pleasing to you, i.e., a photo, a plant, or a candle. If you don't have walls or a desk, wear a pretty bracelet that you can focus on to fill yourself up with joy. If at all possible, leave your workplace during a break or lunch, even if it is only for five minutes. Look around outside, it will fill you back up and give you a whole new perspective at work.

EXERCISES

Look around you. What do you see that makes you feel good? Describe it.

Go in each room of your house and find something that makes you feel good in every room. Describe what you find.

If you can't find anything that you like in your home, write about what you don't like.

Write about how you would like to change what you don't like. It may be as simple as lighter paint on the walls or removing clutter. Write down some action steps you can take to make your home more visually pleasing.

If you work outside the home, find something at work that is visually appealing and makes you feel good. Describe what you see in your workplace that makes you feel good. If you can't find anything, leave your workplace at lunch or at break time and find something joyful outside. What could you bring to work that would give you joy? A ring, a bracelet, a picture?

Have you found your comfort spot yet? How are you progressing towards making it a reality? What do you see from your comfort spot that makes you feel joy? Write about it.

A sight to delight in.

Robert Southey

WHAT DO YOU HEAR?

What do you hear on a regular basis? Do you watch a lot of TV? What kinds of shows do you watch? Is there violence and noise coming from the TV? (You may want to review Chapter 9.)

What words do you hear? Are they words of love and laughter or hate and despair? Pay attention to what people say to you. How can you move away from the negative words and find people that speak more positively? Do you need to reconsider some relationships?

When was the last time words of love were directed at you? Has it been a long time? How do you define "words of love?" Some words of love that you may hear but don't allow into your heart can come in the form of a thank you, a smile, or a shared laugh. Words can have a powerful effect on how you feel about yourself. It is time to honor your Self and be around those that fill you with joy by their words.

Music can be healing and bring great joy. It can be calming or energizing. When you are stressed, you may need some good old rock-and-roll to release your pent-up energy. Sometimes you may need the soft, soothing sound of classical, jazz or new-age. Use music to comfort you or energize you, and feel warmth in your heart.

Do you spend time in silence? Silence is powerful and most of us have too little of it in our lives. Find silence each day, every day, and listen. Breathe into the silence and feel your muscles relax. Enjoy the silence—and the peace and joy it can bring.

What words do you say to yourself? Pay attention to the thoughts that go through your head. Don't be hard on yourself. I often tell my patients if they said the things to their friends and family that they say to themselves, they would have no friends or family around. If you notice a constant flow of negative thoughts filtering through your brain, stop them by thinking of something positive. Instead of "I am so fat" think "I am making healthy choices and moving towards better health."

EXERCISES

Turn off the TV and radio for a day and enjoy the silence. How does it feel? Write about it.

As you go through your day, notice how words of love come to you in different ways. Send out loving thoughts and watch how they come back to you. Write about the words of love that came to you and how it felt to let them into your heart.

Who shows or has shown you love? What words did they use and how did you feel?

What type of music do you enjoy listening to? How does it make you feel? Listen to music every day for one week. The following week, go to the library and check out CDs of different types of music. Which new type did you enjoy the most?

Do negative thoughts flow almost continuously through your mind? Are you switching to more positive thoughts? Each morning, think one new positive thought about yourself, then whenever you start beating up on yourself, switch over to the positive thought. Do this for one week. Write down the positive thought for each day. This takes practice, practice, and more practice. How do you feel when you switch over to that positive thought?

When music fails to agree to the ear, to soothe the ear, the heart and the senses, then it has missed the point.

Maria Callas

WHAT DO YOU SMELL?

Your sense of smell is connected to the part of your brain that holds memories, which is why a certain smell can trigger a wonderful memory or a not so wonderful memory. What do you smell? How do these smells affect you?

Aromatherapy is a form of treatment that utilizes essential oils to stimulate the sense of smell to affect people physiologically and emotionally. One drop of essential oil equals twenty cups of tea—it's powerful stuff.

We often use essential oils to reduce stress in our office. The oils that we use are lavender for relaxation, mint and rosemary for focus and energy, and cedar for cleansing. I mix forty to fifty drops of essential oil with water in a twelve-ounce spray bottle. Whenever any of us are stressed, we grab the bottle and start spraying. Sometimes we spray straight up into the air and take an essential oil shower.

The only essential oils that can be applied directly to the skin are lavender and tea tree. The others should be mixed in some type of carrier oil, such as sweet almond oil, and then massaged into the skin. You should mix three to five drops of essential oil to one teaspoon of carrier oil. Essential oils are pure oils from plants. Perfume oils are not, so make sure you get the real stuff if you want the most effect.

A good stress reducer is to add a couple drops of lavender or vanilla essential oil to your bath, and soak your troubles away. Lavender essential oil can also be used for tension headaches. Apply one drop of oil to each temple, then sit down, relax, and smell the wonderful aroma. (If you use too much lavender you can develop a headache.)

Eucalyptus essential oil has antiseptic and expectorant properties and is wonderful when you have a cold, sinus problem, or bronchitis. My favorite way to use eucalyptus essential oil is to run two to three inches of water in the bathtub. Drop fifteen to twenty drops of the oil into the bathtub and turn on the shower. You have a eucalyptus steamer that will help clear your sinuses and chest cold. You can also put a drop or two into your humidifier. Eucalyptus is also stimulating and can be used to get you moving.

What other ways can you use your sense of smell? How about going outside and smelling the fresh air—or opening the windows and letting the fresh air in? Light a scented candle. Bake. How can you use your sense of smell to invite joy into your life?

EXERCISES

Focus on the various scents you encounter each day. Which ones make you feel good? Which ones don't? How can you add scents that bring joy into your life?

Make a list of your ten favorite scents. How can you bring them into your life?

Write about a scent that stimulates a good memory. How can you bring that scent into your life?

Go to a health-food store and play with the essential oils. What are your favorite scents? How can you use them in your life?

Focus on the aromas while you eat. Which foods smell best? How do they make you feel? Do they stimulate pleasant memories? Write about them.

Nothing awakens a reminiscence like an odour.

Victor Hugo

WHAT DO YOU TASTE?

The sense of taste can get some people in trouble, especially those who use eating as a feeling stuffer. What you eat and taste can bring you joy—or not. Your goal is to pay attention to what you eat and to focus on eating healthy nourishing foods.

Most of us tend to concentrate on foods that are sweet, sour, and salty—why not go for pungent, astringent, and bitter?

Bring excitement to your diet! It takes about eight weeks to get your taste buds used to different flavors, so plan on that amount of time before your body fully embraces the change.

To begin a modification to your diet, first write down what you eat for three days. Also note what time and where you eat your meals and snacks. After three days, review your notes while answering the following questions: How many vegetables and fruits did I eat? Am I eating a variety of vegetables and fruits? How much fast food and processed food do I eat? Was I sitting down when I ate? Was I reading or watching TV? Did I put the food on a plate or in a bowl—or did I just eat it out of its original container? How many sweets did I eat in the course of three days? What did I drink? How much protein did I get? (Protein comes from meat, cheese, nuts, eggs, and soy.) How many carbohydrates did I consume? (Foods high in carbohydrates include bread, pasta, rice, beans, corn, peas, potatoes, and bananas.) After monitoring your eating habits for three days, are you ready for a change?

A protein diet works well for overall health. Instead of starting your day with a caffeinated drink, eat protein. Protein will stabilize your blood sugar and promotes weight loss and clarity of thinking. If you don't usually eat breakfast, start to do so as breakfast is the most important meal of the day. It is called breakfast because you are breaking the fast after not eating all night. You just need a bit of protein to get you started. (One of my patients eats ten walnuts.) You also need to get a large cup, fill it with water, and drink water throughout the day.

There are two symptoms you may encounter when you begin the protein diet (see the References/Resources section in the back of the book for protein diet books). You will go through sugar withdrawal and you may experience constipation. Sugar is a drug and withdrawal will occur when you stop consuming it. The withdrawal process can take anywhere from three days to two weeks. Withdrawal symptoms can include irritability, fatigue, headaches, severe carbohydrate cravings, etc. Don't cave into the withdrawal symptoms. Know they will pass and you will soon feel terrific. (If you experience constipation, take Metamucil with lots of water or Triphala, which is a blend of three Ayurvedic herbs.)

Does going on a protein diet mean you'll never eat sugar or carbohydrates again? Not necessarily. If you tell yourself that you can *never* have chocolate, I guarantee you will end up binging on chocolate. Why? To make up for the rest of your life when you won't be eating chocolate!

Make a daily or moment-to-moment choice to eat healthy. When a craving hits, ask yourself: "If I choose to eat this sugar, how will I feel?" and "What other way can I nurture myself?" You might try to focus on an activity you enjoy to satisfy momentary feelings of deprivation.

Start looking at the food you eat as a *choice*. This will empower you to make healthier decisions. And, when you make healthy choices, congratulate yourself on a job well done, on taking baby steps towards feeling your joy.

If you decide to indulge in a treat, eat mindfully. Revel in the glorious extravagance—savor the indulgence. When you decide to splurge, do it right. Get really good chocolate, or a scrumptious pastry, or an incredibly delicious piece of chocolate cake or premium ice cream. Fill yourself with joy and pleasure as you indulge your sense of taste. You will be filled with pleasure and less likely to do it often. This is how you consciously use your sense of taste.

The more nourishing foods you ingest, the better you will feel and you will have more clarity of mind. This is what life is about. Take care of yourself, treat yourself once in a while, and what spills out from you to those around you is joy. It is time to take back your life and to care for your precious body.

EXERCISES

Write down everything you eat for three days. Evaluate the amount of carbohydrates, fats, and protein you consumed.

When you decide the time is right to make changes in your life, purchase a book, such as *The South Beach Diet* by Aurther Agatson, MD, and start reading it. Evaluate your diet and where you need to make changes. Write down the steps you must take for these changes to become a reality.

After you make these dietary changes, write down how you feel each day. Remember it can take anywhere from three days to two weeks for the sugar withdrawal symptoms to dissipate.

You have moved through the worst of it. Keep on going! Keep on reading.

Indulge in a treat. Eat it mindfully and derive all the pleasure and joy that you can. What did you indulge in? How did it feel to use your sense of taste mindfully?

Take one day and consciously choose what you eat. If something tempts you, say no and honor yourself instead of caving in and feeling guilty. Write about how you felt the next day after you made the choice to eat wisely.

Talking of Pleasure, this moment I was writing with one hand and with the other holding to my mouth a nectarine—good God how fine. It went down soft, pulpy, slushy, oozy— all its delicious embodiment melted down my throat like a large beautiful strawberry.

John Keats

WHAT DO YOU TOUCH?

What is touching you? What are you touching? This sense can bring joy. A loving touch from your lover, friend, or child can fill your heart and soul. Touch can also be devastating when it is done with harmful intention.

What kind of touch is in your life? If you are being physically harmed by another person you need to make a change in your life—now—by moving away from that person. No ifs, ands, or buts. No human deserves to be harmed by another.

Our society is so fast-paced today that not a lot of touch seems to happen. We are always in a hurry. When was the last time you stopped to hug your child, your spouse, or a friend? Try giving a hug to someone today. How did it feel for you? Imagine the impact it had on the person you hugged.

Studies show that touch is imperative to human life. For example, we know that during World War II, orphans that were fed and kept dry, but not touched, died. How much touch is in your life?

If you aren't able to hug someone today—find something that is huggable, i.e., a favorite pillow or a soft blanket. Take it to your comfort spot and enjoy. If you're in the office and need a hug, touch your thumb and second finger together. The energy can circulate through your body and help you feel calm. The more you practice this the better it feels.

How about the sensation of water on your body, whether it's a warm bath, shower, or jumping into a river or lake? Do you like walking barefoot on a sunny beach with the wind blowing through your hair? Pure bliss for some!

Pets can be wonderful to touch. Who can resist a cat curled up on her lap or a dog lying next to her on the floor?

An Ayurvedic technique that can give you the health benefits of touch is a daily massage. If you are of small build, use sesame oil; medium and large women can use sunflower or sweet almond oil. A daily massage has several health benefits, such as increasing vitality, improving circulation, increasing alertness, detoxifying your system, increasing your immune system, nourishing your tissues, and providing a stabilizing influence all day long.

Your head, ears, and feet are the most important parts of

your body for a grounding effect. You can massage yourself first thing in the morning before you shower. Stand on a large towel so the oil does not get on the floor. Beginning with your head, use small circular movements on your entire scalp, rub your ears and behind your ears. Massage your breastbone with up and down strokes; use circular strokes on your chest and abdomen. Try to massage as much of your spine as you can, and use up and down strokes on your buttocks. For your arms and legs use vigorous up and down strokes on the long parts and circular movements on the joints. Vigorously massage your feet from toes to heels, don't forget to massage between your toes. It is important that you massage vigorously and with loving intention. After you are done, hop in the shower and use a mild soap. You will notice an effect on the first day.

You can also have someone else give you a massage. A massage every other week or once a month is a great gift to yourself and to your health.

Pay attention to the different sensations you are able to experience and note those you miss. Bring touch into your life. Touch is an important aspect for bringing joy into your life. Find ways you can reach out to people and touch their lives. This will circle back to you and bring you a warm feeling of joy.

EXERCISES

What touches you that feels good? What touches you that is unpleasant? Can you replace it with something that feels good?

Each day for the next week, give at least one person or ani-
mal a hug. If you can't find anyone to hug, give yourself a big
loving hug. Write down whom you hugged and how it felt.

What objects in your home can you replace with items that
are soft and pleasing to the touch? How about some large
fluffy towels? Look at what you have and dream about what
you would like to have. Write about it or cut out pictures and
paste them in your journal.

Give yourself a daily massage for one week. See if you notice
any difference during the week. Also monitor how you feel
after you have stopped for a couple of days. Purchase cold-
pressed oils from the health-food store.

Get a massage from someone in the next thirty days and
write about how it felt.

Touch is our most important sense.
Without it we would die. Yet we often
neglect this vital source of comfort.

Jennifer Louden

Twenty-Seven

Shoulds and What-Ifs

Shoulds and what-ifs are joy snatchers. I *should* do this; I *should* do that. *What if* this happens; *what if* that happens? You can drive yourself batty and make yourself sick by thinking this way.

When you follow through with something you should do, do you enjoy it? Probably not. How many of your what-ifs come true? Probably not many. It is time to stop *should-ing* and *what-iffing* yourself. Does this mean you don't have to do the things you don't want to? No, but it means you can look at what you need to do in a different light. Does this mean you are going to stop worrying about things? Yes! Giving up worrying is a process, but by taking baby steps in that direction, you can certainly fill your life with more pleasure and joy.

I counsel many women who are exhausted, depressed, and anxious. As they talk about their lives, we discover that their exhaustion, depression, and anxiety are directly related to their long list of shoulds. I also see a multitude of other symptoms, such as migraines and stomach problems, from too much shoulding.

Some common things women *should* about are:

- ◆ I should be a good mother. (Translation: I should do whatever my children want me to do, buy whatever they want, and be there for them whenever they need me.)

- ◆ I should be a good wife. (Translation: I should keep a clean house, cook healthy nutritious meals, and be ready to make love at any time.)

- ◆ I should be a good employee. (Translation: I should always get my work done perfectly, come in early and work late, and never take a sick day.)

- ◆ I should do volunteer work. (Translation: I should help out in my community, even though it takes time away from my family and things that are important to me.)

- ◆ I should take better care of my health. (Translation: I should exercise every day, lose some weight, and take some time for myself.)

Superwoman to the rescue! I can do it all. Does this sound familiar?

What can you do about the shoulds in your life? First, for a couple of days pay attention to how many times you say "I should do that." And notice how you feel when you say this. Then, use the word *could* the next time you catch yourself saying "I should do that" and see how it feels. *Could* implies an option of not doing something—or at the least you can consider your options. Thus, you can say no if it is something you prefer not to do. When you are shoulding yourself, you usually say yes before you think it through.

Am I suggesting you only have to do what you want to do?

No. But you need to be responsible to your Self. If you keep shoulding and trying to do all the things that are physically impossible for one person to do, you will get sick. I see it every day.

You can also feel like a martyr. According to the *American Heritage Dictionary*, a martyr is "a person who endures great suffering" or "a person who makes a great show of suffering in order to arouse sympathy." Are you enduring great suffering or are you punishing those around you with all the shoulds you are trying to live up to? Who suffers in your life when you are doing too many shoulds? A difficult question to answer, but one you might want to look at. Are you starting to feel guilty? STOP! Look at your life and ask yourself, "Where do I want to go from here?"

How often can you say no without feeling guilty or saying, "I should do that"? How often do you say yes, so the other person will be happy, but you end up miserable and stressed out? The way to change this is by learning to say "No", a difficult word for many women. Try it now. Say, "No, I can't do that." How did it feel? Were you able to say it?

It is time to use the word no to save yourself from the stress of living in a world of shoulds.

The other trap you can get caught in is the I-can-do-it trap, thinking it won't take that much of your time. Think again. It will take time and usually much more than you expected, which is time away from what is important to you.

Another technique is to use an accountability person, or AP for short. Your AP can be anyone. It can be your husband, child, or sibling. Your AP is someone who holds you accountable to your life. They are there to ask you the question: "If you take on this activity, what are you going to give up?"

The next time you are asked to do something you really do

not have time for, tell the person making the request that you aren't sure if you can do it; and you'll get back to him with an answer. Then discuss it with your AP. If you know what your AP is going to say, you can just skip the discussion with your AP and call the person back. Then you can say, "I thought it over and I am swamped right now. I would really love to do this project, but I can't at this time." If the person is being pushy, you can explain that you also talked it over with so-and-so (your AP) and they are against you taking on the project.

Is this the wimpy way out? Maybe, but it works. And it is a good way to begin learning how to say no with the support of someone who cares about you. In time, you will be able to check in with your AP in your head and get the answer.

Let's return to the issue of volunteering. My question is, if you are stressed to the max, screaming at your kids, and in poor health, do you think it is a good idea to do volunteer work? I would say no. When you are a mother, you need to focus on your children. When your children are grown and they need less of your time, then you'll be able to help others and give back to your community.

Look at the shoulds and all the times you say yes. Ask yourself how much you can feasibly do in a day without hurting yourself or those around you. Would you expect that much of anyone else? Think about the roles you have every day, i.e., mother, businesswoman, wife, cook, housecleaner, schedule monitor, etc. How many hours do you work in the different roles each day, each week? Ask yourself "Am I having fun?"

Some women look at other women and think, "They can do it all—what is wrong with me?" Number one: different people have different amounts of energy. Number two: you don't know what goes on behind closed doors. Number three: It doesn't matter. Look at your life. Are you feeling joy and pleasure in your daily life? If not, it is time to make some changes and release all the shoulds from your life.

What-ifs are another way to snatch the joy out of life. They are a waste of time and hard on your body. The next time you catch yourself what-iffing, think of it as a red flag, warning you that you're about to go in the wrong direction and you need to change your thought pattern.

Remember, you can only think of one thing at a time—so, the goal is to let go of the what-if and put a positive thought in your head. For example, if you are what-iffing all the bad things that could happen to your child, think of good things that could happen to your child. Imagine your child safe and secure, reaching his or her greatest potential. Thinking positively will make you feel better—and that is what matters. This takes practice and can be difficult to do (read Chapter 18)— but think joy and you will get moments of peace that are wonderful.

Are you what-iffing about not getting all your tasks done in one day? What if I don't get this done? What if I don't get that done? What if this happens? What if that happens? When this occurs, ask yourself, "Will anybody die if I don't get everything done?" Then ask, "What awful consequences will occur if I don't get everything done?" Most likely nothing serious will happen.

The next step is to say a mantra that will calm you: "I have all the time I need." Say this over and over and you will begin to feel a sense of peace, and the more peaceful you feel, the more your mind will clear. You will be able to accomplish much more in a calm, centered manner than if you are in a what-iffing frenzy.

The truth is that you have little control over most events and people in your life. What you do have control over is how you feel about life and the events that occur. If you are spending a lot of time worrying over what could happen, you are not living. You are not living in the present moment. You are also probably not feeling much joy because worry inhibits that feeling. It is time to stop worrying about shoulds and what-ifs and fill your body, mind, and soul with joy.

EXERCISES

Write down all the shoulds in your life.

Pick one of your shoulds and use the word *could* instead of *should*. Does this put a different perspective on it? Evaluate whether you want to do this could. Write about how it feels to use *could* instead of *should*.

Look at your should list again. Are there some shoulds you can let go of? Write down what steps you can take to release them. Be kind to yourself.

Who can be your Accountability Person? Call him or her and ask if he or she will help you with this. Let him or her help you change your life. Write about how it feels knowing you have an AP.

Sometimes it helps if in the morning or before you go to bed at night, you think of one positive thing about yourself or your life that you can focus on whenever you start what-iffing. Write down something good about you and your life.

Take a day or two and whenever you catch yourself thinking negative what-if thoughts, replace it with a positive thought. Whenever you are worried about getting everything done remind yourself: "I have all the time I need." Keep saying this over and over again until you feel it in your heart. Write down how this feels.

Think about a couple of what-ifs that you have about your loved ones. Write down a positive thought about that person that you can think of whenever you start to what if about them.

Don't worry about a thing. Every little thing is gonna be all right.

Bob Marley

TWENTY-EIGHT

Choices

You have the freedom to choose. Sometimes it might feel as though you don't; but in reality you do. You can choose each and every day, each and every moment to invite joy into your life or not. What do you choose?

How are you feeling right now? Take a moment to think about how your day went. If you just got out of bed, think about yesterday. Life can be full of joy; but it can also be difficult for extended periods of time. And minor irritations that occur on a regular basis, can also get you down.

The question is: How are you going to deal with the difficulties and the minor irritations? If you are angry and irritable most of the time because of life's difficulties and irritations, you will not feel joy

For most people, it is not the big stuff that gets to them, it is the day-to-day little stuff that drives them nuts. How often are you irritated on the drive to work? That is not a good way to start the day. How often does something minor happen that sets you off and ruins your day? How can you stop this from happening? Choose to do something different, choose to feel something different.

Life is about choices. It is making a choice on how you perceive what is happening to you on a moment-to-moment basis. Some of my older patients say, "I just don't get that upset about things anymore. It is not worth it." I tell them their wisdom is speaking.

You can fly off the handle about something that you cannot change or you can accept it and let it go. It feels so much better to let it go than to continue feeling bad about something.

Choice is about seeing things in a positive light. One of my patients came to see me about starting menopause. She had just turned fifty. Her youngest child was graduating from high school in a couple of months and another child had recently moved out of the house—my patient was feeling great. She said, "For the first time in my life I can see where my life is heading. I am thrilled to see my children spread their wings and fly in directions that I am excited about. I am looking forward to spending time with my husband without the kids. My job may be ending due to some cuts they are making, but that is okay. I had a job before I had this one, so I know I will find another one."

She wondered if she was all right. She wasn't feeling the empty-nest syndrome that so many of her friends talked about. She wasn't worried about losing her job. Many women had asked her if she was sad about her children moving out. "Not really," she would say. Others would ask, "Aren't you worried about your job and having kids in college?" "No, not really," she would reply. As she told me her story, I could see the light in her eyes (this little light of mine, I'm going to let it shine). She said, "I can see my future, or at least some of it, it looks good and I am eager for it."

She was entering the Wise Women stage in an incredible way. She was making choices that felt good. She could make the choice to curl up in a fetal position and wail "My children are all gone, I am nothing!" Or she could celebrate this new stage of life with her children. She chose the latter. It was exciting to see and I told her she was on the right track. This woman is going through many changes; however, she is choosing to be excited instead of fearful and depressed.

What about the little things, those minor irritations that can send you right over the edge for the whole day? How do you deal with them? It is so easy to make the choice to not invite joy into your life and just muddle through the day. It is so easy to let a minor irritation expand until it has ruined your whole day. It is so easy to see through the eyes of distress rather than eyes of joy. It is so easy to perceive the day as awful, when if you just opened your eyes a bit you would see the joy that surrounds you.

"Not in my life" you say. Take a moment and think about what you have read in previous chapters about inviting joy into your life. What technique can you use to change your perception—to choose joy instead of distress? This can be challenging and it takes practice, practice, and more practice. Why not practice and take the time to invite joy into your life? Why would you choose to let others or certain incidents drag you down for the whole day? How can you choose to see what is positive instead of what is not?

Choice may include moving away from certain people or places that cause you irritation on a regular basis. If every single time you are around someone they bother you, make a choice. Choose to not be around that person, or choose to focus on what you like about that person.

What would your life be like if you magnified the good and forgot to look for the bad? When you make the choice to find the good in people, you will see some awesome things. When you keep making the choice to feel joy, more and more joy will come your way. You have a choice in how you react to the world. It is time to take charge of your life and make the choices that feel good to you and bring you joy.

EXERCISES

How are you feeling right now? What are you feeling good about or what are you feeling bad about? Write about how your day went or how yesterday went. Were you mostly feeling good or mostly feeling irritated?

If you mostly felt good, wonderful! If you were mostly irritated, how can you change that around and choose to feel good? Write about what you could feel good about.

Think about something significant that bothers you. What can you do to make the choice to feel joy about this situation? In other words, what can you find good about this situation? You may not be able to find joy in the situation— but you can move away from the irritation that you feel. Write down what bothers you and one or two points that are good about the situation. If you are in the middle of a big life change, take a moment to look away from the event to something in your life that brings you joy. Write about what brings you joy.

Write about something that causes you a minor irritation on a regular basis. Write about how your body feels when you are irritated. Write about what you can do to change this situation from one of irritation to one of joy. Remember, it is how you perceive the situation that causes you to feel irritation or joy. How can you choose to look away from the situation or find compassion within yourself for the situation?

Make the intention that you will choose to invite joy into your life as often as possible through one entire day. Whenever anything happens that doesn't bring you joy, make the choice to change your perception and feel joy. Write about how it feels to be able to choose joy instead of distress. You may be surprised at how difficult this can be at times. Practice, practice, practice and it will get easier.

Take another day and make the choice to invite joy into your life all day. Was it easier this time? Did you encounter challenges that took away the joy? Did you laugh at those challenges and say, "I choose JOY"? Did you feel joy when you did this? Write about how this day felt.

♡

You can close the windows and darken your room, and you can open the windows and let light in. It is a matter of choice. Your mind is your room, do you darken it or do your fill it with light?

Unknown

TWENTY-NINE

Order

Most people are surrounded by chaos, which is why they usually feel stressed. What happens in your environment affects how you feel on the inside. When you live in chaos, your body, mind, and spirit are in chaos. If you are in a calm environment, your body, mind and spirit can feel a sense of peace.

According to the *American Heritage Dictionary*, *chaos* means "any condition or place of total disorder or confusion." Does this sound like your home? When there is disorder there is confusion, and where there is confusion there cannot be joy. How can you let go of the disorder and confusion in your life and bring order and joy back in? If you live with anyone, especially children under the age of five, this can be challenging. If you live alone, there are no excuses.

Let's get started.

This is going to be a long-term project and the number of people in your home will be a factor to consider. If you have young children and are making yourself crazy trying to keep your house clean—stop, it's not worth it. All you are doing is spending a lot of time making yourself crazy and not spending time with your kids. Confine their toys to a couple of rooms and let them be. You can also consider how much stuff your kids really need. Anything they don't play with is just taking up space. Get rid of it. (This is best done while they are sleeping.)

One complaint I hear is grandparents giving grandchildren too many gifts. Maybe it's time to sit down with the grandparents and explain that you are trying to bring order into your life. You can make a list of the things your children need, and then ask the grandparents to stick to the list. If they don't, there is always Goodwill or a garage sale. If the thought of this conversation makes you nervous, think about this: Your being nice and not saying anything is making you crazy. This is your home and you can decide how to raise your children.

For those of you who don't have young children, you can start by cleaning out the garage or basement. How much stuff have you accumulated that you haven't looked at in a year—or years? Do you even know what is in those boxes?

As you look around, you may feel overwhelmed. This is normal. Bringing order into one's life is not often talked about. We are a society that is constantly seeking more stuff. We hate to get rid of our old things because we may need them some day. But we have to put it somewhere, so we shove it in a box and take it to the basement, the attic, or the garage. It is amazing how much you can accumulate in a short amount of time. It is time to clean out the mess. Take a deep breath and get started.

There are several ways to bring order to your house. You

can dedicate one day a week to clean one area. You can do one task per day. The main thing is to begin and set a time for cleaning. Once you have decided where you will begin and when you will do it, write it on your calendar. You need to be firm with yourself—and committed.

As you sort through the stuff, make three piles. One is junk, to be thrown out; another is for Goodwill or a garage sale; and the last one are things you can't part with. Set a date for your garage sale so the items don't sit in the garage for the next year or so. Anything that doesn't sell at the garage sale should be taken to Goodwill.

After you have finished the first room and, most importantly, enjoyed your accomplishment, it is time to pick the second room. Will it be the garage, the kitchen, the bathroom? You choose, and then begin. Continue doing this until you've gone through the entire house and garage. Remember, this is a long process. What you are looking for is lightness. Order. Joy will follow. Chaos comes from having too much stuff in your environment. Simplicity promotes a sense of calmness. Calmness allows that feeling of joy to come through.

Sarah Ban Breathnach's book, *Simple Abundance*, can help you through this process. And *Simplify Your Life* by Elaine St. James is another excellent book about bringing order to your life.

A final thought. If you live with people who do not value neatness, bringing order into your home can be a huge challenge. You may have to take over a spare room and not allow anyone to enter it. (See Chapter 3.) It may mean that you only clean the basement and the garage for the time being. You may need to develop a plan and enlist the help of the people you live with.

There is an old saying: "If Mama ain't happy, no one is." If you are feeling crazy because your home is a mess and no one is helping out, this is a bad thing. If you come home from work and find your house a disaster area and your darling children and spouse sitting around, the rage you feel is a long way from joy. That rage will eventually come out, and it won't be pretty. Suppressed rage is even more harmful, because it hurts you. I love what Sue Monk Kidd says in *The Dance of the Dissident Daughter*: "Rage implies an internalized emotion, a tempest within . . . What rage wants is to move outward toward positive social purpose, to become a creative force or energy that changes the conditions that created it. It needs to become outrage." Honor that rage. We, as women, feel bad when we become enraged so we tend to quickly stuff it back inside, where it just builds up again. Begin to look at your rage as outrage at the circumstances that you find yourself in and let it move you towards making changes that work for you.

It is time to make a plan of action and get your loved ones to help you. As order returns to your home, joy will return to you. When Mama is happy, everyone is happy.

EXERCISES

Walk through your house. Make a list of what needs to be done. This will be your checklist to check off as you complete each little project.

What amount of time are you going to devote to bringing order to your life each week? Will it be one small task per day, a couple of hours once a week or an entire Saturday? Write down your plan.

Do you need to enlist the help of those that live in your home? Write out a plan of what you want and what your expectations are of each family member. Hold a family meeting to discuss your plan and ask for input. Set a date to begin your plan of action.

Write down how it feels after you have completed the first room. You could even take a picture of before and after.

♡

Without order
nothing can grow or expand.

Unknown

THIRTY

Taking Care of Your Self

The way many women live has nothing to do with them at all. When I talk to my patients about finding time to eat right, get some exercise, and take time to do something they like to do, they simply say they can't. They are too busy taking care of everyone else and there's no time left for them. This is sad—and unhealthy.

In order to take care of others, you must take care of your-self. It begins with baby steps. Review your weekly schedule. How many people and activities are you involved with each week? What is one thing you can give up each week and replace it with time for you? What is one thing that you can delegate to someone else so you can have time for your Self?

I remember watching a Phil Donahue show several years ago. It was about women complaining about how little men did around the house. Phil's point was that if women did it all, men were not going to beg to be allowed to wash the dishes, do the laundry, or mop the floor. I have thought about this periodically. How often do you complain and yell as you are doing all the housework—but never get any help? How often do you sit down with your family, in a calm and objective way, and lay out a plan of action that requires participation by all members of the family?

I can hear some women say, "It is easier to do it myself." My point is, then do it yourself—but if you want their help, you will have to change your approach. People, especially your loved ones, will use you up then ask for more on a daily basis. It is time for you to stand up and say, "I can do no more. I need time for me."

Now that you have given up one activity a week, what can you give up on a daily basis? Where can you find time on a daily basis to do something for you? This takes planning. Remember the 5 Ps: Prior Proper Planning Prevents Problems. You are changing your life. Take your time, look around, and see what you want to do. Go back to Chapters 5 and 6. Have you found time to do some of the activities that you like to do? How much time do you spend in your comfort spot? Now is the time to start making a plan to bring those activities that are important to you into your life.

How do you want to spend your life? Do you want to spend your life doing for everyone else but your Self? If so, you will become exhausted, depressed, and eventually bitter. This is no way to live. Include a bit of yourself in your life each and every day and move towards a feeling of joy. As you take care of yourself, that feeling of joy radiates out from you—and everyone around you benefits.

EXERCISES

Look at your schedule for the week. Can you find your Self in the schedule? What can you give up each week, each day? How can you live your life instead of everyone else's?

Alert those around you about the activities you are giving up. Devise a plan of action to have those around you help out with the day-to-day activities. Remember the 5 Ps: Prior Proper Planning Prevents Problems. Schedule a meeting to discuss your plan.

Write down one activity you can do daily or weekly that will make your life more pleasant. At the end of the week write about how it felt to focus on your priorities. Make sure you don't set yourself up for failure by trying to do too much. Remember, take baby steps.

Make a sign that says "NO!" or "I can't do that at this time as I have other commitments" and place it near your phone. Use this sign. Write about how it felt to say No! the first time and the fifth time. As you do this, remember the twenty-four-hour rule. If you do something that is not on your priority list, you take away from what is really important to you. Next to the NO! sign, place your priority list, so you remember why you are saying no.

♡

*It is one thing to decry the rat race . . .
That is the good and honorable work of
moralists. It is quite another thing to
quit the rat race, to drop out, to refuse
to run any further . . . that is the work
of the individualist. It is offensive because
it is impolite; it makes the rebuke
personal; the individualist calls not his
or her behavior into question, but mine.*

Paul Bruchow

THIRTY-ONE

Anger

♡

If you are angry, you can't feel joy. If you feel joy, you can't feel anger. Women have been socialized to not get angry. We are supposed to be nice. When we aren't nice, it is our fault. The problem is, we do get angry. We might suppress our anger or even have ourselves convinced we don't get angry—but we do—and it can eventually come out in a rage directed at an innocent party and over something that is insignificant. Then we feel bad. We feel guilty and we start suppressing all over again.

What you need to do is learn how to give voice to your anger. You need to acknowledge your anger when it arrives instead of letting it build up until your voice turns into a bellow. You need to look at what makes you angry and speak to that instead of turning your anger on innocent parties. You need to stop saying, "Oh, not a problem" or "I can do that," or

"Don't mind me, I'm just fine" until it does become a problem or you can't do it or you are not fine. You need to listen to your gut.

It has been a powerful discovery for me to reflect on the events that occurred before I "overreacted." Many times I was not being heard or listened to. I asked several times, nicely, and was totally disregarded. As time went on, the anger started building and I "overreacted." Begin to look at what is underneath your "overreactions."

How many times have you been nice to someone that was mean to you? Do you keep going back for more, just to be nice? How does it manifest itself in your body? Do you rage at somebody else, do you get a migraine, a backache, or diarrhea? When does it become time to say, "Enough is enough, I will not accept this behavior anymore"? When does it become time to let the anger rise to the top and say STOP? Oftentimes women take what they would never give to another human being. We take what we would never allow to happen to our loved ones. We take until we are full of suppressed anger—and then we wonder why we feel no joy.

How often do you suppress your anger to keep the peace? Learning to deal with your anger means learning to speak your truth. Get a journal and write about what upsets you. Be honest. Do this for three or four months and see what the pattern is. (If you are still menstruating, this is best done during PMS time, the two weeks before your period. You will want to call your best friend and tell her where the journal is. If anything happens to you she is to go immediately to the journal, destroy it, then find out how everyone is doing. This way you can be absolutely and completely honest about what is irritating you.) It may be that you are tired of picking up after your family. You may have a friend who is always bringing you down. Your boss may be taking advantage of you. You may find that you just want some time to yourself.

Once you have established what is wrong, do something about it. Make a plan and implement it. (If you are still menstruating, this is best done from the time you start your period until two weeks before your period.) If you deny yourself, the rage will only intensify. Implementing a plan takes time and working with the people around you. It requires holding your own and not being pulled back to the way you were—and others will pull you hard. It takes looking at what makes you angry and saying, "NO MORE!"

As you release the anger your shoulders will loosen, your lower back pain will dissipate, your bowels will work on a regular basis, your migraines will disappear, and your children won't live in fear of you. You will begin to rediscover the simple pleasures of living and joy will be a part of your daily life.

EXERCISES

Pay attention to when your rages occur and at whom. Write down this information. Ask yourself if you are raging at the appropriate person. If not, who is the appropriate person? Write about this person and what you really think of this person.

What consequences can you set for this person's actions? Write them down. Carry them through and write about how it felt. If your nice girl starts to come out, write about what you would do if this was happening to someone you loved.

If you are still menstruating, journal during your PMS time. Write PMS after the date. After three or four months read what you have written during your PMS time. It can be an eye-opening experience. What are you going to do about this situation that keeps coming around every month? Make a plan and implement it during the two weeks before PMS begins. Write down your plan.

Listen to what you are telling your daughters, sisters, and girlfriends about being nice. Is it the same thing you would tell your sons, brothers, and male friends? Write about the differences.

The next time you overreact, take some time to reflect on the events that led up to your overreaction. Write about them and how you could do things differently.

♡

Anger is a signal
and one worth listening to.

Harriet Lerner

THIRTY-TWO

Sleep

Sleep, glorious sleep. When was the last time you had a good night's sleep? When was the last time you woke up feeling refreshed and leapt out of bed to greet the day? Sleep deprivation, in my mind, is a form of torture. Over time, not getting enough sleep can lead to depression.

We are a country of chronically sleep-deprived people. We have too much to do every day and not enough time to do it. We stay up late, then wake up early and do it all over again.

When do you go to bed? In Ayurvedic medicine it is suggested that you go to bed around 10:00 p.m. "That's too early, you say. I'll miss the eleven o'clock news." Personally, I don't think murder and mayhem (which usually dominates the news) is a healthy prelude to a good night's sleep.

What do you usually do right before bedtime? Do you work to the point of exhaustion, and then fall into bed? Do you eat before bed and go to sleep with a full stomach, then wake up two hours later with indigestion?

When you get to bed, does your mind wander and do your thoughts keep you awake? Do you wake up in the middle of the night and then can't fall back to sleep?

Let's start with what you do before bedtime. If you stay up late to watch the news, stop doing this for two weeks. Try going to bed at 10:00 P.M. and see how you feel in the morning. Then, return to watching the eleven o'clock news. Do you notice any differences?

Don't eat anything after 7:00 P.M. According to Ayurvedic medicine, our digestive fire is weak in the evening, which causes food to sit in our stomachs and can lead to indigestion. Eat a good dinner and sip some tea later in the evening if you are hungry—or rather, if you think you are. If you think you are hungry, ask yourself what you really want other than food. Evenings are the best time for eating when you aren't hungry.

Stop working until bedtime. Try relaxing for an hour or so beforehand and see how you sleep. Even if you have too much to do, you will never get it all done—and if you get a good night's sleep, you will function much better the next day. How can you relax? Read, work on a hobby, or watch a funny movie. This may be a time to do some spiritual reading in your comfort spot. If you are unable to sleep, write in your journal to empty your mind.

Is your bedroom dark, peaceful, warm enough, and quiet? Are your sheets soft? Do your blankets keep you warm? Do you have a good mattress? All of these factors will help you be comfortable so you can get a good night's sleep.

You are now snuggled in bed. Take a deep breath; your day is done. Let yourself drift off to sleep. If your mind insists on running nonstop, you may want to get up and do some more journaling. Another technique is to use imagery. This will need to be worked through during the day to prepare you for the night. You will want to think of a place that you love and use your five senses as you imagine yourself there. This gives your mind something to think about and can cause you to relax and drift off to sleep.

As you lay in bed, focus on each one of your senses for a short while, then move onto the next. If your mind races away to think about something that happened during the day, gently bring it back to your special place. The more that you practice this, the easier it gets.

Some people may need help falling sleep. My favorite herb is Valerian. (In Europe it is called the "herbal valium.") It can shut down your thinking and help you drift off to sleep. Valerian is not addicting. For some people, it may work right away. For others, especially if you have long-term sleeping problems, you may have to take it for a while to feel any effect. Melatonin can also be helpful for sleep, especially if you have long-term sleep problems. Melatonin, a hormone in your body, decreases as you get older. Its main function is to help you sleep. It generally takes a while to build up in the body before it works. Give Melatonin six to eight weeks before you decide if it is working or not.

A hot bath can be relaxing, especially if you add a couple drops of lavender essential oil. Scientific research has discovered the mechanism of why a hot bath works: a hot bath warms up your core body temperature, which helps you sleep. It was found that people who had a cooler core body temperature did not sleep as well as when they were able to warm up their core body temperature. Take a warm relaxing bath before bedtime and see if you don't improve your sleep habits.

There are a variety of herbal teas you can buy to help settle you so you can sleep. Two herbs that are helpful for this are chamomile and passionflower. You may also try a cup of warm milk with a half-teaspoon of nutmeg.

Are you waking up in the middle of the night and then unable to get back to sleep? As women age, this is more likely to occur. Melatonin can alleviate this problem. If you are waking up because you are having hot flashes, you may need to seek professional help. You can try herbs, but if they are not strong enough you may need medication for a period of time.

Sometimes a foot massage with a couple of drops of peppermint essential oil can keep you cool and allow you to sleep. It is fairly common for peri-menopausal women to go through a phase where they cannot sleep the night through. I suggest trying some of the above remedies to see if they help.

If you are waking up with indigestion, you should look at your eating habits. Of course, there are medications available to reduce the symptoms of indigestion but it's best to go to the source of the problem. I have seen indigestion or GERD (gastro esophageal reflux disease) completely clear up in one day to two weeks on the protein diet. Try it; you will be amazed.

Another important aspect of getting a good night's sleep is the time you wake up in the morning. If you get up late, it will interfere with your day and your night. In Ayurvedic medicine it is recommended you wake up no later than 6:00 A.M. If you stay in bed after six, you enter what is called *Kapha* (earth and water) time. This is a slower time and will cause you to enter the day in a sluggish manner. If you get up at 6:00 A.M. or earlier, you are in *Vata* (air) time and will enter the day with good energy. Wake up earlier and see the results; you might be surprised. (A gradual change by setting your alarm fifteen minutes earlier every week until you hit six is suggested.)

Can you catch up on your sleep? Yes, but it is better to do

this by going to bed earlier rather than sleeping in later. According to circadian rhythms, it is better to get up at the same time with no greater deviation than one hour from the time you normally get up. So, if you wake up at 6:00 A.M. during the week, you should wake up no later than 7:00 A.M. on the weekends. Therefore, to catch up on your sleep, you need to go to bed earlier.

After a long week, it is okay to give yourself permission to go to bed early. You will have much more energy to do what you need to do if you get extra sleep one night a week. Try it. You may wake up feeling great and energized.

Have you ever taken a nap? It can feel quite decadent. Some days I like to take a power nap for about fifteen minutes after work. Relaxing into a nap on a Saturday or Sunday afternoon can also feel wonderful.

Sleep is a wonderful activity. Sleep deprivation leads to depression and chronic fatigue, which drains the joy out of you. Make a commitment to yourself to get some good sleep and watch those feelings of joy return.

EXERCISES

Go to bed at 10:00 P.M. and get up at 6:00 A.M. for two weeks. If you need to move towards six by setting your alarm fifteen minutes earlier each week, do so. Write down how you feel at the end of two weeks. How did it feel to give up the evening news for two weeks?

Try some of the remedies in this chapter. Write about the ones that improved your sleep.

Use imagery at bedtime or when you wake up in the middle of the night. Write about your favorite place and define what you see, hear, smell, taste, and feel. Write about how effective imagery was for you.

Take a hot bath before bedtime. Add a couple of drops of lavender essential oil. Did you sleep better?

Look at your bedroom. Is it warm, quiet, dark, comfortable, and peaceful? If not, what changes can you make? Write about them and how you can make them happen.

Sleep is better than medicine.

Unknown

THIRTY-THREE

Balance and Responsibility

In the United States we are rewarded for being busy, and for working and playing hard. Many times, though, we run out of hours before we can play. We must be responsible; otherwise we are seen as frivolous. However, if you don't bring some balance and fun into your life, you will experience no joy. Remember, all work and no play makes Jane a dull girl. It can also kill Jane.

How much responsibility are you taking on? Who and what do you feel responsible for? Do you feel responsible for your spouse? What about your children? How old are they? Are you still taking responsibility for their lives, even though they are old enough to be responsible for themselves? How much does this responsibility throw your life out of balance?

How are things at work? Do you find that you take on others' responsibilities? It is interesting to contemplate the thought that when you do not allow others to take responsibility for themselves you are stunting their growth. If you do not let others take responsibility for themselves, they will never feel the excitement or satisfaction of doing it on their own.

Of course, there is a transition period between you letting them go and their taking on the responsibility. This can be a difficult time for both parties. Ultimately, though, people must take responsibility for their own lives and decisions. Children must be allowed to make mistakes and figure out their lives. If you are always there to pick them up, they will never learn. Can you give them love and compassion? Absolutely. Can you control their lives? Absolutely not. It only makes you tired and doesn't allow them to grow.

I saw a new patient the other day. She was having problems with increasing anxiety and fatigue. The medications she was on were not working. As we talked about her life, she told me her son and his fiancé, both in their twenties, were living with her. They had a large dog that was making a mess of her home. Her son and fiancé argued a lot, which caused her distress. Plus she was doing their laundry and cooking all of the meals. The young couple did not help out in any way around the house.

She was used to being nice and didn't want to hurt their feelings by asking for help. She never had time to do what she wanted to do. In fact, she was late for her appointment with me.

I told this woman she was getting too old to take care of her adult children. She needed to talk with them about doing their share of the household tasks. I sent her to a counselor to help her work through this. I also asked her to take some time for dancing, an activity she loved, but hadn't made the time for.

Children will allow you to do everything for them until you

say, "No more." It is not easy to do this; but it must be done for your self-preservation and for their growth.

It is time for you to allow people to take responsibility for their own lives. This will free up some time, so that you can take responsibility for your life. You may be called selfish when you start to release the responsibility of others. Ignore it. In most cases being called selfish just means you are not doing what other people want you to do for them. Finally, you are doing something for you—at long last. This self-preservation is greatly needed by many women.

Once you've relinquished responsibility for others, you can ask yourself "Am I living a life of balance?" Imagine yourself on a tightrope. How does your life stack up? Is there anything on the fun side? Is the work side fully loaded with things to do and lots of responsibility? How can you change this and bring more balance into your life? What can you let go of? What might you add on the fun side?

Having a balanced life and allowing others to be responsible makes your life joyful. There is no joy in being responsible for others when they should be responsible for themselves. There is no joy in a life that is so out of balance you are doing nothing for your Self. Bring some balance to your life and let yourself be filled with joy.

EXERCISES

Watch for circumstances, at home and in the office, when you are doing something that someone else should be responsible for. How can you give that responsibility back to the person in a loving, compassionate way? How can you prevent yourself from taking back that task if you don't feel the person is taking appropriate responsibility? Ask for help from a friend or counselor, or pray for help to prevent yourself from taking back the responsibility. After you have worked on this for a while, what other responsibilities can you release to the appropriate people? Write about how it feels to release the responsibility, how hard it was to not take back the responsibility, and how proud you are of yourself that you didn't take back the responsibility.

Make two lists, one on the right side of the page and one on the left side. In the middle, draw yourself. On one side of the page, write what you are responsible for. On the other side of the page, write what you do for you that is fun.

Look at your list of responsibilities and choose one to release. Write it down. Then write down how you are going to release this responsibility. Sometimes it helps to discuss it with the person in a calm, objective way. Yelling at the top of your lungs that you are not doing this anymore is usually not effective.

Now that you have released some responsibility, look at your fun side. Pick one fun activity and write it down. Then write down how you are going to bring this fun into your life. Write down how it feels when you start doing the activity. This is how you begin to invite joy back into your life.

Write down another responsibility you can let go of. Write down how you are going to do this. Are you starting to see the fun in this?

*If a man insisted always on being serious,
and never allowed himself a bit of fun
and relaxation, he would go mad or
become unstable without knowing it.*

Herodotus

Thirty-Four

Detachment

What are you attached to that is not bringing you joy? How can you detach from those things? The simple answer is to just let it go, to release it from your life, to detach from it. The problem, sometimes, is that it keeps coming back.

There are a couple of different techniques you can use to detach from that which does not bring you joy. The techniques are defining what matters and what does not matter. These techniques take time and practice; but they do work.

First, is there someone you are attached to that constantly irritates you? How often do you find yourself complaining about a particular person's behavior? "I cannot believe they did that to me." "I cannot believe they are doing that." Can you hear yourself thinking or saying this? Have these thoughts ever changed how that person acts towards you? Absolutely not. What they have done is make you miserable and taken the joy out of your life. It is time for detachment, to cut the cords and release these thoughts from your mind and life.

My brother handles people like this by telling himself it doesn't matter. When he realized there would always be people he couldn't change, even if they irritated him, he knew *his* outlook had to change. He could do nothing about the situation, and in the grand scheme of life, what that person was doing didn't matter because there was nothing he could do to change them or the situation. So, whenever he caught himself ruminating about something, he filled his head with the thought "It doesn't matter," and let it go.

This is wise advice. When you start to complain about something or someone, detach from the miserable feelings by saying, "It doesn't matter." Eventually this will become a habit and you may be surprised at how much negativity is released from your soul.

When you empty your mind of something that doesn't matter, a space empties in your head. Fill it with thoughts that do matter. Then the negative thought can't return quite so easily. It might return at another time, because that is the way our minds work, but with continued practice you will focus on what does matter and stop thinking about what doesn't.

Let me give you an example. Let's say you have a new boss who is making some changes you do not like. There is nothing you can do to prevent the changes. So, you do what most of us would do in this situation—you complain a lot. Complaining will get you absolutely nowhere, except feeling miserable. This is when you remind yourself it doesn't matter. Change will always occur—at the office and at home. At times like this, focus on what is good instead of the changes you cannot control. It can be helpful to make a list of the things that do matter. If you are having problems at work, what is good about your job? If you are having problems at home, what is good about your family? The more you look for what matters, the more things you will find. Try it; it is amazing how a shift in perspective can change how you feel.

Detachment is hard and it takes practice. It takes realizing that you must accept people as they are. It takes the desire to feel joy instead of misery. It takes releasing what you cannot control and focusing on what brings you joy What are you holding onto so desperately that makes your life miserable?

I had a dream where I was holding on for dear life to two handles embedded in a wall. I knew if I let go, something terrible would happen to me. Finally, the thought occurred to me to just stand up and let go, so I did. As I stood up I felt firm ground underneath my feet. An incredible feeling of relief came over me as I let go of what I was so desperately holding onto. The joy I felt as I released those "handles" was incredible. Can you stand up and release the negativity that you are holding on to and focus on what really matters?

Pay attention to your thoughts. See if you can catch yourself ruminating about someone else's behavior. Try thinking it doesn't matter and release it. Remember you cannot change someone else's behavior. You will only make yourself miserable. Next, think about what does matter. Fill your heart and soul with thoughts about what matters and allow joy into your life.

EXERCISES

Think of a person or situation that regularly makes you miserable. Then tell yourself it doesn't matter. "I cannot change this person's behavior. I can only change my reaction to their behavior." How does it feel to say this?

Make a list of things that matter, specific to a situation that doesn't matter. See how many things you can come up with that matter, compared to the one thing that doesn't matter.

Choose a friend to play the "it doesn't matter" game. Help each other when one of you starts to complain about situations or people you cannot control. Write down how it feels to change your thoughts to what really matters in life.

Imagine every person in the world is enlightened but you. They are all your teachers, each doing just the right thing to help you learn perfect patience, perfect wisdom, perfect compassion.

Jack Kornfield

Thirty-Five

Guilt

My spiritual director once told me that guilt is a good thing. Huh? She explained that when people feel guilty, they are in transition. "Will you continue to do what you have been doing or will you use the guilty feeling to go in a new direction that will empower you?" she asked.

In *Conscious Loving*, Gay and Kathlyn Hendricks define guilt as "a mixture of anger and fear." You are angry because you are doing something you do not want to do but are fearful that if you don't do it that person won't like you anymore. Guilt is a red flag that indicates you are doing something for someone for the wrong reasons. You are giving this service out of fear and you are denying yourself, once again, which causes the anger. Guilt is an uncomfortable feeling; but when looked at as a transitional phase, can empower you and help you begin to invite joy into your life. Guilt is good.

As I thought about guilt and began to talk with my patients about guilt, I saw how devastating guilt can be to one's life. I saw many instances where guilt made people completely give up their lives to care for others.

Burt Goldman states: "More than any other emotion, guilt puts a heavy burden upon us, both spiritually and mentally. Guilt is laid upon our shoulders by many authority figures . . . for two reasons, to control and/or to punish."

When someone asks you to do something and you say no, do you automatically feel guilty? If yes, why? Should others control your life? How many people in your life punish you for saying no in small, passive/aggressive ways? Anyone? How many times after you say no, do you feel so guilty that you change your mind and do what you said no to—just to assuage your guilty feelings? How do you feel when you do the task? Probably not so good as there is likely to be a bit of animosity for feeling coerced into doing it.

What toll does this type of behavior take on you over the long term? Seriously consider the answer to this question. Sometimes, in the short term, you will feel good about changing your mind—but the long-term consequences of always doing for others and not yourself will catch up with you and surface in rage or illness.

The most expert guilt givers are those that are closest to you—like your children. It can also be your spouse or your parents.

One of my patients worked fulltime; had two young, active kids; a husband; and a home that required all of the usual care. During our conversation, she said, "I don't want to disappoint my children." Wow!

How much do we do for our children that, over time, causes us to crash and burn? I suggested to the woman that we do have to disappoint our children. Otherwise they will suck us dry and then ask for more. It is their way and we are the only ones that can stop them.

The parents of my generation were pretty tough. They had lives of their own and didn't seem overly concerned about disappointing their children. Parents of today, however, don't have lives of their own and cater to their children exclusively. And so, the pendulum swings. We need to get back to the middle ground where we have a life and still provide good care for our children.

How many women feel guilty if they take time for themselves? How often do women yell and scream at their children and/or husbands because they don't take time for themselves? Why do we believe that we can give and give and give and never fill up? Guilt.

After contemplating the idea that guilt is good, I came up with a strategy: When you feel guilty, you have to make a choice. Do you do what this person wants you to do or can you be true to your Self and do what is right for you? It is as simple as that.

When you do something you don't want to do out of guilt, you won't feel joy. You will feel bad. To make the right choice, you must stop, look at the situation, and check in with how you feel.

Imagine yourself at a crossroads. Do you take the left, which will have you doing what the other person wants or do you go to the right and do what feels good to you? As you're standing at the crossroads, look at the choices objectively. Is the request reasonable? How do you feel about the request? Do you really want to do what you are being asked to do? Do you want to go back to the old habit of taking care of everyone but your Self?

If you do this, will you be so stressed out and irritated that you yell and scream at your kids, or get sick?

If you continue to do things out of guilt, people will suffer. First it will be you, and then it will be those around you. When you explode, you won't be addressing the issue or necessarily the person who made the request. You will get angry about something inconsequential that will make you feel even guiltier because you erupted. Then you feel bad, apologize, and the issue behind the explosion is never addressed or discussed.

Are you ready to move into a different way of being? Are you ready to care for yourself? By choosing the right path, you are saying you are ready. You won't know where you are going, because you haven't been there yet. It may be uncomfortable at first, but it is time to strike out in a new direction and be good to your Self.

The next time you feel guilty, examine the situation. Is this an old pattern of behavior that causes you to do what everybody else wants you to do? Do you want to go down that path again or would you like to try something new? Will you always be able to do what feels good to you? Unfortunately no; but you must do some things that make you feel good.

Realize that when you start changing your behavior, those around you will probably not applaud. They like having you do everything for them. They will pull you hard, trying to get you back on the wrong path. Hold firm, it is all right for someone to be mad at you. If they are mad, think about *why* they are mad. Is it because you are doing something for your Self and not them? Probably. Is that how you want to live your life, always doing for others and never you? There is no joy in that kind of life.

You may want to refer back to Chapter 27 on finding an Accountability Person. Having a support person as you work through releasing yourself from doing things out of guilt can be helpful and soothing to the soul. You may also want to refer to Chapter 17 and think about what you would suggest to your best friend if she were in the position you are in. Then, follow your own advice.

As you make changes, consider whether or not you are giving service to someone—or have you become a slave to that person? There is often much bondage in the name of service. When you give service, you are coming from a full heart with a sincere desire to help. When you are in bondage you are being forced to give service. This force generally comes from inside influences, such as feelings of guilt.

When you agree to help someone, are you giving service from a full heart (and it feels good) or have you fallen into a role of servitude and it does not feel good? In a slave role, your heart is empty because all you have done is give and give and there is nothing left in you to give. Your tank is on E. It is time to take the road to the right, release yourself from bondage, and do what is healthy for you.

Do you feel guilty about something that happened long ago? If you do, apologize for what you did. The other person may or may not have forgotten. When you feel guilty about something you did in the past, you need to make restitution for what you did, and then let it go. Release it from your life so the joy can return.

How do you make restitution? You can phone the person or send them a letter. If you don't know how to contact the person, write them a letter and then burn it, to release your guilty feelings. You may want to do a public service for someone who is in the same position as the person you hurt. Forgive yourself for making a mistake, just as you would forgive another person who has made a mistake.

Sheila Quinn Simpson has written a beautiful book entitled *Apology: The Importance and Power of Saying "I'm Sorry"*. If you are feeling guilt over something that you have done, this book can lead you through the process of making amends. As you move through the process of making an apology, you can release your guilt and even possibly change someone's life. Apologizing from the heart to another person is a powerful act of love. It can change your life, and help you release your guilt and the awful feelings that go with it. Apologizing can release you to find your joy.

You cannot do it all. You cannot be all things to all people. It is not physically, emotionally, or spiritually possible. You must look at guilt straight on and realize that when you don't give in to it, you can begin rediscovering the simple pleasures of living.

EXERCISES

The next time you feel guilty about something, stop for a moment. Tell yourself guilt is good. Sit with that for a moment. Envision a crossroads. How will it feel if you turn to the left and do what is asked of you? How will it feel if you turn to the right and do what feels true to your Self? Know that the first time you choose to do what is good for you, it will be hard. You can do it. Write about how difficult it was to do what was right for you. The next time you do something that is right for you, write about it. Keep doing it until you reach your tenth time. Have you made any progress?

Call your Accountability Person for support. Think about how you would advise your best friend if she were in a similar position and then follow your own advice.

The next time you help someone, ask yourself: "Am I coming from a position of service or bondage? Am I coming from a full heart or an empty heart? Do I feel good about giving this service or am I doing it out of guilt?" Do this in several situations, so you can feel the difference between giving from a place of joy compared to one of guilt. Move away from those services you give out of guilt.

Make restitution to someone for something you feel guilty about. Write about what you did.

Show me a woman who doesn't feel guilty and I'll show you a man.

Erica Mann Jong

THIRTY-SIX

Gratitude

When you pay attention to your life, you can find many things to be grateful for. This means staying in the present moment and being open to the abundance of gifts that come your way. Most days you probably don't even see them; so slow down, look, and take a few moments to appreciate what is going on around you.

What one thing brings you pleasure? Do you have a comfortable home? Loving children? A steady job? A supportive spouse? Good health?

Finding pleasure in your life takes work. It is much easier to think about what brings you dissatisfaction than what brings you satisfaction. As you practice finding things to be thankful for, more good will come your way. And, you will want more of this joy and, therefore, look for other things for which to be grateful. Eventually, dissatisfaction will be something you experience less and less.

The present moment is the best place to find these gifts; though you can also look into your past or future. It's easiest to be appreciative of the small things in life. In the present, open your eyes and see what is around you. What do you love about your home, your relationships, and your work? If you have little or nothing that brings you pleasure, it is time to make some changes in your life. How often do you say "thank you" for the gifts you receive?

When you experience gratitude, not only does it feel good, it also helps your body heal—you feel joy.

Take a closer look at what surrounds you. You may need to begin with the basics, like the shoes on your feet. Imagine if you didn't have shoes. Your feet would be cold; you would have to walk across stones and dirt, and maybe even snow. That would be miserable. Now, let a warm feeling of satisfaction enter you for those wondrous shoes on your feet. Doesn't that feel good?

Does this seem silly? At times, it can be. You may even need to fake it at first. But the more often you do, the better you will feel. This is joy and it is what you are working towards feeling all the time. As you go through difficulties and tough transitions in life, you may need to envision where you would like to be and what brings you delight. Your future can be brighter, if you believe.

A technique that helps you find something to feel better about on bad days and increases the amount of pleasure you experience is writing in a Gratitude Journal. Keep this journal in a visible place and write down at least one thing you are grateful for at the end of each day. When you write about something it makes it real and it will also help you think of other things that can fill you with gratitude. When you have a hard day, you can look at what you have written in your journal and bring back those good feelings. The Gratitude Journal is a reminder of the blessings that come into your life on a regular basis.

Some days writing in a Gratitude Journal can add stress to your life. If this is the case, don't do it on that particular day. I remember a time when I would say, "I have to write in my Gratitude Journal." I would get my journal and think *What am I grateful for?* and write down each thing as quickly as possible. I did not have any feelings of pleasure; thus my effort was a waste of time. The pleasant feeling is the most important part.

Another way to increase your delight is to share what you are thankful for with a friend. It should be a special friend who is also working towards finding gratitude in his or her life. When you share what is good in your life, it feels wonderful. Remembering what is enjoyable is helpful in getting through a grueling day or a difficult moment. Put your attention on what good things you have in your life instead of the challenges that you are going through at the moment.

Another way to feel grateful is to say "thank you" for the blessings you receive every day. How often do you say "thank you" for the good things that come your way, especially those you asked for? How often do you notice them? When you realize the gifts you receive, say "thank you." Tell your friends about this and encourage them to pay attention, too.

Also, notice the manner in which gifts come to you. The more you say "thank you," the more often gifts will come. Give it a try.

Saying "thank you" for all the little things that come your way can feel so good, if you allow it. Giving thanks for the difficulties that come your way can be harder, but try that, too. Behind every challenge there is a lesson to be learned. That lesson can lead to greater things. Or, as Michael Mirdad, PhD, said in the *Creating Fulfilling Relationships* workshop I attended, "The Universe will call you to healings." I rather like that thought. It feels so much better than "learning a lesson" or "being hit over the head with a two-by-four." As you look underneath the difficulty and allow a healing to occur, gratitude can surface.

As you feel gratitude for what you have, your life will fill with joy.

EXERCISES

Make a list of ten things you are grateful for.

Spend one day looking for things to be grateful for. Write them down and describe how you feel when you give thanks for them.

Purchase a gratitude journal and a pretty pen. Write down one thing you are grateful for each day for a week

Find a friend you can share your blessings with. Every day for one week share something that you are grateful for.

Pay attention to your day and see what gifts come your way. Don't forget to say thank you. Write down what you received. Think back to when you asked for it. Marvel at the interesting way it came to you. Have fun.

Take some time to look at a difficult event in your life. Is there a lesson or a healing that you can take from this difficulty? Has this difficult event moved you back on to your true path? Journal about what you came up with. If you have a good friend that you can discuss this with, a powerful healing can occur as you look deeper into the issue and the meaning it has on your life.

If the only prayer you say in your whole life is Thank You, that would suffice.

Meister Eckhart

Thirty-Seven

Are You Being True to Your Self?

♡

By the time you reach this chapter, hopefully you have worked on discovering what brings you joy. It takes effort to find and keep joy in your life. Are you inviting joy into your life on a daily basis? How can you stay true to your Self and begin to rediscover the simple pleasures of living?

How often do you give and give and give and then find there is no time left for you? How often do you do what society dictates and then feel empty inside? How often are you being untrue to your Self?

You have worked through this book and discovered what brings you joy. Now, look at your life and see how many of these things you have brought into your life. Realize this is not a time when you beat yourself up because you have brought so little into your life. Honor where you are and what you have done. If you have not done much, that's okay.

Review the notes you made. What is stopping you from bringing joy into your life? How can you let some of those things go, so you can start being true to you?

When you think about doing what you want, different arguments can come to mind and stop you in your tracks and cause a moral dilemma. "I should help this person. It will only take a couple of phone calls, a little bit of time here and there. I am supposed to serve other people, etc."

What will serving others cost you? Once again—no time for you. I see many women's lives on a continuum. They are so busy helping people; there is never any time for them. If this is still where you are, go to the extreme left and take care of your Self. As you begin to be true to your Self and feel good, you can move back to center. At the center is balance: taking care of your Self but also helping one or two others.

How does it feel to start being true to you? It can feel terrible. Guilt will settle in and you may move back towards being untrue to your Self. In *The Invitation*, Oriah Mountain Dreamer writes: "I want to know if you can disappoint another to be true to yourself; If you can bear the accusation of betrayal and not betray your own soul."

These are powerful words. Can you stand in your truth and not be swayed by what others want you to do? Can you listen to your quiet inner voice that says, "It is too much. I can't do this. I need to say no." Can you listen to that quiet voice and follow what she says? As you transition, you will feel guilt. Take a moment now and look at that guilt. Ultimately, it is either you or them. Which do you choose? Will you be true to your Self and start moving towards a joyful life?

EXERCISES

Pick a day and observe where all your energy goes. How many people have you taken care of during the day? Write down whom you took care of and what you did for them.

Pick a couple of things from that list and think about how you can let go of those tasks. Write down what you came up with—and do it. Then write down how it felt to let go of serving other people. If guilt enters in, remember it is you or them. Choose you.

Pick another day. Every time you are asked to do something, pause for a moment. Ask yourself, "If I do this task, will I be true to me?" Write about what you said no to and how it felt.

As you whittle away at the multitude of obligations you have taken on, use the techniques you have learned to bring more joy into your life. How does it feel to have time for joy in your life on a regular basis? Write about what you are doing to bring joy into your life. Write about how you are being true to your Self.

Trust yourself, You know more than you think you do.

Dr. Spock

THIRTY-EIGHT

Joy or Reality

♡

"You're not living in reality." "You have to be realistic." When you start living in joy, people may say this to you. Your response can be: "I like my happy world. You can join me or not."

What is reality? Reality is serious; it is believing nothing is possible. It is looking at the practical aspect of everything. Reality can be a dream killer. It is seeing the world as a dangerous negative place. Fun and play are not allowed when you live in reality. Some people live in reality all the time. They are generally competitive and are always trying to prove themselves. They are quick to point out other people's faults. Fear is an element that they live with on a daily basis. They don't have a whole lot of fun and they miss out on all the magic and joy around them.

Sometimes you will get jerked into reality because of outside circumstances. It may be the loss of a loved one, a divorce, losing a job, or a health issue. You wake up one day and the whole world has changed. Everything is different.

When this happens, as you walk through this change, you can ask: "After going through this tragedy, who am I? What are my strengths and weakness? How do I want to be from this day forth?"

Can you figure this out overnight? No, it takes time—a lot of time—to look at this reality and move yourself back to your bliss, to your joy.

Sometimes reality is required to help you redefine yourself—and to grow. It can be unpleasant, but it is worthwhile if you take the time for it. As you walk this new path, you can find your bliss again, and feel joy bubbling up in your body. You will smile and laugh again.

When you are living in your joy, the world is a magical place. You will use the many techniques discussed in this book on a regular basis. It does take effort and time to do these activities. But it is worth it. This is where you get to choose joy or reality. Do you want to take the time to invite joy into your life? Or will you allow the joy snatchers to snatch any pleasure from your life?

EXERCISES

Do you live in reality every single day? What have you learned from this book that may move you towards your joy, at least once in a while? Pay attention to what other people are doing who live in joy. Can you learn something from them? Write about what you can do to invite joy into your life.

Have you just gone through a tragedy and been jerked into reality? Write about what you are going through. Write about what this reality feels like.

Write about how you can honor your Self as you go through this transition. You may need to use the step-out-of-yourself technique discussed in Chapter 17. What would you tell your dearest friend who was going through the same thing? Write about your response.

Write about the joy snatchers in your life and what you are going to do about them so you can return to your joy.

Take a day and make a choice to live moment-by-moment in joy. What techniques did you use throughout the day? Write about the day.

Choose to live each day in joy. When reality strikes, honor it and your Self. Ask for help to make the changes you need to make. Take the time to do this. Find little bits of joy and pleasure each day as you walk this new path and know that, in time, you will move back to your joy.

♡

*I believe in looking reality straight
in the eye and denying it.*

Garrison Keillor

Thirty-Nine

The Joy Break

How can you get in the habit of finding joy during your day? Try taking a joy break. What is a joy break? It is taking a moment to stop and feel joy. It is as simple as that.

To do this, you must establish a habit. Generally, it takes twelve weeks to set a habit. The easiest way to begin developing a habit is to set a time, write a note, and then do it. You may decide that every day at 10:00 A.M. you will take a joy break. Write it down on your calendar. At 10:00 A.M., do it; don't blow yourself off.

What can you do during your joy break? You may want to pick a different technique each day or you may want to do the same thing for a week. You choose, but do it. It is so easy to procrastinate. "I'll do it tomorrow. I don't have time right now."

Make the commitment to implement the ideas and exercises in this book in your daily life. By taking a moment each day to practice what you have learned, these new habits will soon become a part of you. As you invite joy into your life each day, your life will change. When life hands you a lemon, you will know how to make lemonade instead of becoming a sourpuss.

As you find your joy, you make the choice to be true to your Self. When you are true to your Self on a regular basis your heart, soul, body, and mind start to heal. You move towards becoming the person you were meant to be—a person living in joy.

EXERCISES

Take a joy break for seven days in a row. Write down what you did and how you felt. Notice if you feel differently at the end of the week.

Do it again for another week.

Keep doing this for the next ten weeks. Note how you feel now and how you feel at the end of ten weeks of taking joy breaks. Note if you continue to take more joy breaks as the weeks progress.

Joy is the feeling of grinning on the inside.

Dr. Melba Colgrove

THE TAO OF JOY

Joy abides, she does not hide
Joy unfolds, she never holds.
Joy sets free, she does not flee.
Joy invites, she never fights.

Joy ascends, she always blends.
Joy allows, she always bows.
Joy lets go, moves with the flow.
Joy always shows the way to go.

~ SANDRA HINES

Notes

CHAPTER 1: THIS LITTLE LIGHT OF MINE

Walsch, Neale Donald. *The Little Soul and the Sun*. Charlottsville, VA: Hampton Publishing Company Inc., 1998.

CHAPTER 2: SOLITUDE

Estés, Clarissa Pinkola. *Women Who Run With Wolves*. New York: Bantam Books, 1999.

Thomas Gray, *Elegy Written in a Country Churchyard* (1751), line 73 retrieved September 6, 2006 from Alexander Huber, editor; *The Thomas Gray Archive*, The University of Oxford Press; www.thomasgray.org.

CHAPTER 11: RELATIONSHIPS

Richard Bach. *Illusions, The Adventure of the Reluctant Messiah*. New York: Dell Publishing, 1977.

Oriah Mountain Dreamer. *The Invitation*. San Francisco: Harper Collins Publisher, 1999.

Howard Thurman quoted by Sam Keen. *Fire in the Belly*. New York: Three Rivers, 1997.

CHAPTER 23: PUTTERING

Jean Shinoda Bolen. *Goddesses in Everywomen*. New York: HarperPerennial, 1984.

CHAPTER 29: ORDER

Sue Monk Kidd. *Dance of the Dissident Daughter, A Woman's Journey from Christian Tradition to the Sacred Feminine*. San Francisco: HarperSanFrancisco, 1992.

CHAPTER 35: GUILT

Gay Hendricks & Kathlyn Hendricks. *Conscious Loving, The Journey to Co-Commitment*. New York: Bantam Books, 1990.

Sheila Quinn Simpson. *Apology: The Importance and Power of Saying "I'm Sorry"*. Gaylord MI: Balcony Publications, 2005.

CHAPTER 37: ARE YOU BEING TRUE TO YOUR SELF?

Oriah Mountain Dreamer. *The Invitation*. San Francisco: Harper Collins Publisher, 1999.

Bibliography and References

BOOKS

Atkins, Robert C. *Dr. Atkins' New Diet Revolution*. New York: M. Evans and Company, Inc., 2002.

Bach, Richard. *Illusions, The Adventures of the Reluctant Messiah*. New York: Random House Inc., 1977.

Ban Breathnach, Sarah. *Romancing the Ordinary*. New York: The Simple Abundance Press, 2002.

——. *Simple Abundance, A Daybook of Comfort and Joy*. New York: Warner Books Inc., 1995.

Bolen, Jean Shinoda. *Goddesses in Every Woman*. USA: Harper Colophon, 1985.

Boorstein, Sylvia. *Don't Just Do Something, Sit There*. San Francisco: Harper Collins, 1996.

Borysenko, Joan. *Minding the Body, Mending the Mind*.

Brockway, Laurie Sue. *A Goddess is a Girl's Best Friend*. New York: Perigree Book, 2002.

Cameron, Julia. *The Artist's Way*. New York: G.P. Putnam's Sons, 1992.

——. *Walking in This World*. New York: Jeremy P. Tarcher/Putnam, 2002.

Duerk, Judith. *Circle of Stones, Women's Journey to Herself*. Philadelphia, PA: Innisfree Press, Inc., 1989.

——. *I Sit Listening to the Wind, Women's Encounter Within Herself*. Philadelphia, PA: Innisfree Press, Inc., 1993.

Eades, Michael R. & Eades, Mary Dan. *Protein Power*. New York: Bantam Books, 1999.

Estés, Clarissa Pinkola. *Women Who Run with Wolves*. New York: Ballantine Books, 1992.

Fischer-Rizzi, Susanne. *Complete Aromatherapy Handbook*. New York: Sterling Publishing Co., Inc., 1990.

Gawain, Shakti. *Meditations*. Novato, CA: New World Library, 1997.

Grabhorn, Lynn. *Excuse Me Your Life is Waiting*. Olympia, WA: Beyond Books, 1999.

Hicks, Esther & Jerry. *Ask and It Is Given, Learning to Manifest Your Desires*. Carlsbad, CA: Hay House Inc. 2004.

———. *The Amazing Power of Deliberate Intent*. Carlsbad, CA: Hay House Inc. 2006.

Hendricks, Gay, Ph.D. & Hendricks, Kathlyn, Ph.D. *Conscious Loving, The Journey to Co-Commitment*. New York: Bantam Books, 1990.

Kidd, Sue Monk. *The Dance of the Dissident Daughter, A Women's Journey from Christian Tradition to Sacred Feminine*. San Francisco: HarperSanFrancisco, 2002.

———. *When the Heart Waits, Spiritual Direction for Life's Sacred Questions*. San Francisco: HarperSanFrancisco, 1990.

Levan, Susie. *Meditations for Healing Stress*. Orlando FL: North Light Productions, 1996.

Lindbergh, Ann Morrow. *A Gift from the Sea*. New York: Pantheon Books, 1955.

Louden, Jennifer. *The Women's Comfort Book*. San Francisco: HarperCollins, 1992.

———. *The Women's Retreat Book, The Comfort Queen's Guide to Life*.

Mander, Jerry. *Four Arguments for the Elimination of Television*. New York: William Morrow and Company, Inc., 1978.

———. *In the Absence of the Sacred*. San Francisco: Sierra Club Books, 1991.

Monaghan, Patricia. *The New Book of Goddesses & Heroines*. St. Paul, MN: Llewellyn Publications, 2000.

Moravec, Kathryn. *Life's Little Lessons*. Fairfeild, IA: Sunstar Publishing, Ltd., 1999.

Mountain Dreamer, Oriah. *The Invitation*. New York: HarperCollins Publishers Inc., 1999.

Myss, Caroline. *Anatomy of the Spirit*. New York: Harmony Books, 1996.

———. *Sacred Contracts*. New York: Harmony Books, 2001.

Northrup, Christiane. *The Wisdom of Menopause*. New York: Bantam Books, 2001.

———*Women's Bodies, Women's Wisdom*. New York: Bantam Books, 1995.

Rose, Jeanne. *The Aromatherapy Book, Applications and Inhalations*. Berkley, CA: North Atlantic Books, 1992.

Schlessinger, Laura. *Bad Childhood, Good Life*. New York: HarperCollins Publisher, 2006.

Schulz, Mona Lisa. *Awakening Intuition, Using Your Mind-Body Network for Insight and Healing*. New York: Harmony Books, 1998.

Sichel, Deborah & Driscoll, Jeanne W. *Women's Moods, What every Women must know about Hormones, the Brain, and Emotional Health*. New York: William Morrow and Company, 1999.

Simon, David. Vital Energy, *The 7 Keys to Invigorate Body, Mind,& Soul*. New York: John Wiley & Sons, Inc. 2000.

———. *The Wisdom of Healing*. New York: Three Rivers Press, 1997.

Simpson, Liz. *Awakening Your Goddess*. London: Gaia Books Ltd., 2001.

Simpson, Sheila Quinn. *Apology: The Importance and Power of Saying "I'm Sorry"*. Gaylord, MI: Balcony Publications, 2005.

St. James, Elaine. *Simplify Your Life*. New York: Hyperion, 1994.

Stassinopoulos, Agapi. *Conversations with the Goddesses*. New York: Stewart, Tabori, & Chang, 1999.

Taylor, Robert; Seton, Susannah; and Greer, David. *Simple Pleasures*. Berkeley, CA: Conari Press, 1996.

Walsch, Neale Donald. *The Little Soul and the Sun*. Charlottesville, VA: Hampton Publishing Company Inc., 1998.

Wauters, Ambika. *Life Changes with the Energy of the Chakras.* Freedom, CA: The Crossing Press, 1999.

Weil, Andrew. *Breathing, The Master Key to Self Healing.* Boulder, CO: Sounds True, 1999.

Woolger, Jennifer Barker & Woolger, Roger J. *The Goddess Within.* New York: Fawcett Columbine, 1989.

Worwood, Susan. *Essential Aromatherapy.* Novato, CA: New World Library, 1995.

Worwood, Valerie Ann. *The Complete Book of Essential Oils and Aromatherapy.* San Rafael, CA: New World Library, 1991.

WEBSITE

"The Secret" Prime Time Productions 2006, www.thesecret.tv

Index

Quick Order Form

Order here or from your leading bookstore.

EMAIL ORDERS ~

mary@maryseger.com

POSTAL ORDERS ~

Send check or money order made payable to *Mary B. Seger* to:
Mary B. Seger ✧ P.O. Box 1924 ✧ Gaylord, MI 49734

Name _____

Address _____

City _____ State _____ Zip _____

Phone (_____) _____

Email address_____

PLEASE SEND THE FOLLOWING BOOKS ~

	QUANTITY	EACH	TOTAL
Invite Joy Into Your Life *Steps for Women Who Want to* *Rediscover the Simple Pleasures of Living*		**$18.95**	
Finding Your Joy ~ *a journal*		**$14.95**	

	ORDER TOTAL
Michigan address ~ add 6% **SALES TAX**	
	SUBTOTAL
Refer to chart at left for **SHIPPING**	
	TOTAL

2007 SHIPPING RATES

SUB TOTAL	SHIPPING
$20 and under	$ 5.95
$20.01 - $40	$ 7.95
$40.01 - $60	$ 9.95
$60.01 - $80	$11.95
$80.01 - $100	$13.95
$100.01 - $120	$15.95
$120.01 - $140	$17.95
Over $140	$19.95

INTERNET ORDERS ~

Visit **www.maryseger.com** to place orders online
through PayPal.